# THE
# FLEET AIR
# ARM
## IN CAMERA

# THE
# FLEET
# AIR ARM
# IN CAMERA

ARCHIVE PHOTOGRAPHS FROM THE PUBLIC RECORD OFFICE
AND THE FLEET AIR ARM MUSEUM

# 1912–1996

ROGER HAYWARD

FOREWORD BY
REAR ADMIRAL T.W. LOUGHRAN
FLAG OFFICER NAVAL AVIATION

SUTTON PUBLISHING
IN ASSOCIATION WITH THE PUBLIC RECORD OFFICE

First published in 1996 by
Sutton Publishing Limited · Phoenix Mill
Thrupp · Stroud · Gloucestershire · GL5 2BU

A catalogue record for this book is available from the British Library

ISBN 0 7509 1254 5

 ™ ALAN SUTTON™ and SUTTON™ are the trade marks of Sutton Publishing Limited

Typeset in 11/15pt Baskerville.
Typesetting and origination by
Sutton Publishing Limited.
Printed in Great Britain by
Butler & Tanner, Frome, Somerset.

# CONTENTS

# FOREWORD

REAR ADMIRAL T.W. LOUGHRAN
FLAG OFFICER NAVAL AVIATION

The history of aviation in the Royal Navy has not always followed a smooth course but, throughout the last eighty-five years, airmen in dark blue have never shirked their duty. As Flag Officer Naval Aviation I preside over a highly-trained, highly motivated arm which forms an essential and integral element of Britain's sea power. However it was not always thus.

*The Fleet Air Arm in Camera* provides a striking series of images depicting the naval air arm's equipment and operations during the only century to experience two world wars. The First World War prompted the pioneering and pivotal achievements in developing the techniques of flying from the fleet, and of creating an offensive capability for its aircraft. The Second World War brought a growing awareness that the aircraft carrier and its squadrons could supplant the battleship as the cornerstone of the Fleet.

Even in the periods of so-called peace, there has rarely been a time when naval aviation was not called upon. From controlling piracy in the South China Seas, through Korea, Suez and Borneo (two campaigns where the helicopter proved its worth to naval air), to the most recent conflicts of the Falklands, the Gulf and Bosnia, the FAA has responded to a wide variety of operational demands and has never been found wanting.

Roger Hayward has unearthed a fascinating catalogue of photographs from all of these periods and created an invaluable narrative on a remarkable band of men and their machines.

Terry Loughran
Yeovilton 1996

# INTRODUCTION

A large proportion of the files and other records passed to the Public Record Office (PRO) by the armed services, the Ministry of Defence and its forebears and a number of other government departments contain photographs relating to various aspects of British naval aviation. Indeed, the PRO's holdings are so extensive in this area that it has not yet proved possible to catalogue more than a small proportion of them. This book has therefore been prepared in the hope of encouraging the general public, together with historians, authors and researchers, to dip into this Aladdin's cave.

The present volume illustrates the whole period of British naval aviation from the first tentative steps in 1912 to the operations and new equipment of the mid-1990s. The photographs have been selected to give a taste of the vast range of material available and the breadth of subjects covered in the records, but they are not intended to provide a comprehensive illustrated history. It would have been inappropriate, and indeed impossible within a work of this size, to illustrate every single aircraft-carrying ship, or every naval aircraft or major event.

Nevertheless, each decade unfolds in pictures and all major conflicts are given due weight. The contribution of the Commonwealth has not been forgotten, nor has that of ordinary individuals, and both success and tragedy come into the tale.

Anyone interested in exploring the records for themselves may apply for a reader's ticket at the PRO, for which formal means of identification will be needed. The PRO is located at Ruskin Avenue, Kew, Richmond, Surrey TW9 4DU and is served by the District Line of the London Underground. Identifying those documents which may contain photographs of naval aviation subjects is not always a straightforward process, but perseverance is infinitely rewarding, and in any case staff are available to offer advice and assistance. Readers may identify documents of possible interest from the class lists to the records; there is also an extensive but as yet incomplete catalogue of photographs housed in the archive. Documents can then be ordered on a simple computerised system, and items can be selected for copying by the Direct Copying section, on payment of a fee.

Copies of photographs are available for commercial reproduction from the PRO Image Library, telephone 0181 392 5255. Prices are given on request. Records held in the PRO, whether photographs or other archival material, are, of course, Crown Copyright and their use is subject to clearly defined regulations.

Information about the PRO and its collections is available in the form of a series of printed leaflets. Examples are: General Information Leaflet No. 15, which discusses Crown Copyright matters; No. 19, which explains the process of ordering copies of documents and photographs; Records Information Leaflet No. 49, which explains how to locate documents relating to the operational records of the Royal Navy during the First World War; and No. 99, which describes the contents of the photographic catalogue. Because the process of providing information to readers is constantly being expanded and updated, reference numbers may change from time to time. However, advice is always available on request. Readers who wish to carry out research for the period up to 1965 are recommended to purchase a copy of PRO Readers' Guide No. 8, *RAF Records in the PRO*, by Simon Fowler, Peter Elliott, Roy Conyers Nesbit and Christina Goulter (PRO Publications 1994), available from the PRO shop. This guide includes an appendix listing other sources of aviation photographs.

One general note of caution has always to be sounded regarding access to the nation's archives housed in the PRO. The provisions of the Public Records Act mean that records less than thirty years old are not normally available for public scrutiny. Therefore it was necessary to select another photographic collection to complement the PRO's material in providing coverage from the mid-1960s to the present. The Fleet Air Arm Museum proved to be the ideal partner, as its collection of photographs, held at the museum at Royal Naval Air Station Yeovilton, Somerset, is unrivalled. We are fortunate in that the Director of the FAA Museum unhesitatingly agreed to participate in the production of this volume. Their collection is equally wide-ranging and some of their photographs have been selected to supplement the illustration of the early parts of the story as well as the last thirty years. Copies of FAA Museum photographs, to which the museum holds copyright, may be purchased by members of the public, authors and publishers while information is available to enquirers in writing or by telephone on 01935 840565. Visitors to the FAA Museum are welcome to view albums from the museum's collection by prior arrangement.

Britain's naval air service has undergone more than its fair share of name changes over the years. Having begun as the Naval Wing of the Royal Flying Corps on 13 April 1912, it became the Royal Naval Air Service (RNAS) on 1 July 1914. It was amalgamated with the RFC on 1 April 1918 to form the new Royal Air Force. A further change occurred on 1 April 1924, when the sea-going element became the Fleet Air Arm of the Royal Air Force. The term Fleet Air Arm has remained in use ever since, although between 24 May 1939 (when the Admiralty regained control of naval aviation from the Air Ministry) and 1953, its title was officially, but never generally, the Air Branch of the Royal Navy.

The system of numbering flights and squadrons of aircraft also altered from time to time. During the First World War, the RNAS operated a series of numbered land-based squadrons, as well as large numbers of water-borne and ship-borne aircraft. There were, in addition, such diverse machines as armoured cars and airships. When the RAF was formed, the landplane squadrons had to conform to the RFC/RAF numbering system and therefore added 200 to their numbers to avoid duplication. Major contraction followed the end of hostilities, and on 1 April 1923 the ship-borne squadrons were redesignated as flights in the 400 series. The situation was reversed in April

1933, when most of the flights became full squadrons in a new 800 series. This part of the reorganization was completed in July 1936, when the remaining flights became squadrons in the 700 series. This arrangement remains current.

The 240 or so photographs which form the backbone of the book have been selected on the basis of being interesting in their own right, forming a coherent sequence that tells the story of the Fleet Air Arm, and as being representative of the two photographic collections. In a few cases, the importance of a photograph's content has been allowed to override the usual considerations of quality. The captions are based as far as possible on the information in the original PRO documents or in the FAA Museum's records. However, this is supplemented where necessary by research in other records held by the PRO and the FAA Museum, from other published sources, and from the author's own archives.

# ACKNOWLEDGEMENTS

The production of this book has been very much a team effort. Many people have assisted in various ways in helping to pull all the threads together. Firstly, I should like to thank Rear Admiral T.W. Loughran, Flag Officer Naval Aviation, for agreeing to write the Foreword. Oliver Hoare of the Public Record Office has been helpful and uncomplaining in answering many queries, offering advice and locating elusive records. Of the many other PRO staff who have assisted, I should like to mention Simon Fowler, Jo Matthews and, for photographic services, Brian Carter. Indeed, it was Simon who sportingly accepted Roy Nesbit's suggestion that I should be invited to produce this volume. Mr D.J. Staerck, a private historian, provided helpful advice about armoured cars. Graham Mottram, Director of the Fleet Air Arm Museum, agreed unhesitatingly to link his museum to the PRO in backing this venture. Among the other helpful and always-cheerful staff at the FAA Museum, David Richardson has not only produced first class material from the museum's extensive collection in response to the vaguest of requests, but has also, on more than one occasion, anticipated my own thoughts. Special thanks are due to David Brown, Head of Naval Historical Branch, and Ray Sturtivant, a leading authority on Fleet Air Arm matters, for agreeing to check the extended captions, and I am grateful for their helpful advice. Any remaining errors are my own responsibility. Finally, I should like to thank my wife for her forebearance with my preoccupation over the last twelve months.

Roger Hayward
Slough
Berkshire
July 1996

# TRIALS AND THE TEST OF WAR

Flying from Royal Navy warships was pioneered aboard HMS *Africa*, a 'King Edward VII' class pre-dreadnought battleship of 15,700 tons. HM Dockyard Chatham installed a long wooden ramp sloping towards her prow from the forward turret, and from this on 10 January 1912, Lieutenant C.R. Samson RN made the epic first flight from an RN ship in this Short-modified S.27 box-kite No. 38. The development was unpopular with traditionalists, as it had the major disadvantage of rendering *Africa*'s fore 12-in gun turret unusable.

FAAM ref: SHORT /289

Further early trials took place on HMS *Hibernia*, also of the 'King Edward VII' class, again using the same type of aircraft. This photograph was taken at Sheerness, with work on the long ramp apparently still going on.

FAAM ref: CARS H/49

A most significant event occurred at 0600 on 2 May 1912, when Lieutenant Samson flew the Short-modified S.27 from the ramp on *Hibernia* while she was underway at 10½ knots in Weymouth Bay – the first take-off from a Royal Navy ship at sea. Samson's own flying log book confirms the event, which took place a full week before the similar well-known take-off during the Royal Review on 9 May.

FAAM ref: CARS H/124

The small (35,000 cubic ft) unarmed Willows No. 4 non-rigid airship was hastily purchased by the Admiralty for the Naval Wing of the Royal Flying Corps in 1913, as it was the only civilian machine available. Known as Naval Airship No. 2, it was transferred to the newly-formed Royal Naval Air Service on 1 July 1914. With only 35 h.p., it proved underpowered and unsuitable for anything but training. After it was withdrawn in 1915, the envelope was used for SS (Submarine Scout) 1. It is seen here lying in Odiham Natural Shelter, a chalk pit which is still a prominent feature beside the main road running past RAF Odiham.

PRO ref: AIR 1/728/176/3/38

With the realization that an aeroplane could be damaged by its own bombs, live tests were conducted to determine the effect of such blasts on the stability of an aircraft overhead. For these, the Maurice Farman S. 7 Longhorn No. 72, modified without the characteristic forward elevator as a floatplane and powered by a 70 h.p. Renault engine, was used to overfly the detonations on 12 December 1913. The last and largest explosion, the splash from which can be seen at the bottom of the photograph, was from 40 lbs of explosive (roughly equivalent to a 112 lb bomb), with No. 72 flying over it at 350 ft. The plane experienced only a slight shock and was not 'unsettled'.

PRO ref: AIR 1/645/17/122/324

Seized from the Germans in 1914, the SS *Aenne Rickmers* of 4,083 grt was taken into service as a seaplane carrier in January 1915, and like many early mercantile conversions, she could accommodate four aircraft. She was present at the bombardment of the Smyrna forts that year; she was torpedoed there and towed to Mudros, where this photograph was taken.

PRO ref: AIR 1/479/15/312/239

This sad wreck is the remains of a Sopwith Admiralty Type 807 seaplane from HMS *Ark Royal*, 7,080 tons, which was converted from an incomplete merchant vessel. No. 808 was being flown by Flight Commander H.A. Williamson and Flight Lieutenant W.H.S. Garnett when it crashed on 5 March 1915 after its propeller disintegrated at 3,000 ft while attempting to cooperate with the battleship *Queen Elizabeth* during the Dardanelles campaign. The Type 807 was popularly known as the Sopwith Folder, as it used the patent Short wing-folding system. The national markings are the early white-red-white pattern.

PRO ref: AIR 1/479/15/312/239

Sopwith Schneider No. 1438, seen here being hoisted on one of *Ark Royal*'s cranes during the Dardanelles Campaign, is particularly interesting as it has a bomb rack fitted between the floats. This is the third production Schneider, the triangular fin and wing-warping in lieu of ailerons being hallmarks of early machines. No national markings are visible.

**PRO** ref: AIR 1/479/15/312/239

The Short Type 166, although designed as a torpedo-bomber, was not used in that rôle. However, it proved useful as a wireless-equipped reconnaissance aircraft for bombardment spotting. No. 161, seen here in a rare flying shot during a test flight over Mudros, was the first of the series and wears an interesting wave-effect camouflage.

PRO ref: AIR 1/479/15/312/239

These two superb photographs show Wight Type A 1 Improved Navyplane No. 176 wearing an interesting camouflage scheme. No. 176 is seen coming alongside *Ark Royal*, ready for hoisting. *Ark Royal*, commissioned on 9 December 1914, could carry up to ten aircraft.

PRO ref: AIR 1/479/15/312/239

No. 176 being hoisted inboard on *Ark Royal*, showing clearly the bomb rack between the floats. The Navyplane pusher seaplane was a large floatplane with a 63 ft wingspan and was used for reconnaissance.

PRO ref: AIR 1/479/15/312/239

Short 135 No. 136 and a Wight A 1, both with their wings folded, on board *Ark Royal* off the Dardanelles just prior to 27 April 1915, when No. 136 was hit by enemy fire and partially sank. It had been considered the best of *Ark Royal*'s eight mixed floatplanes, the only one which could operate in bad weather. The boat-like object in the right foreground is a spare float for the Wight.

PRO ref: AIR 1/479/15/312/239

New equipment for *Ark Royal*. The fuselage of a Sopwith Admiralty Type 860 is being uncrated amid some merriment. This was another intended torpedo-bomber which proved suitable only for reconnaissance.

PRO ref: AIR 1/479/15/312/239

The RNAS was at the forefront of armoured car operations during the First World War, just as the RAF was during the 1930s. The original Armoured Car Squadrons of the RNAS (Aeroplane Support) became the Royal Naval Armoured Car Division, comprising fifteen squadrons. This is car No. 1 of Section C, 5 Squadron, one of the three squadrons with Lanchester cars. It is armed with a Vickers 0.303-in machine-gun in the turret, augmented by a portable Lewis gun. The sloping frontal armour afforded slightly better protection than the flat plates on the better-known Rolls-Royce cars. These were robust and successful cars, capable of up to 50 m.p.h. They served in France and Russia.

PRO ref: MUN 5/394

This formidable beast is a standard Seabrook armoured lorry; car No. 14 of Section B, 5 Squadron. It appears to be well protected, with armour over the chain-drive transmission and rear wheels, and is heavily armed with a naval 3–pounder gun and at least one Vickers machine-gun. The body was designed by the RNAS and mounted on an American Standard Truck Co. chassis.

They were intended to support the armoured cars in their five squadrons, and served in France and the Middle East, but they were slow, underpowered and suffered from weak rear suspension. The ensign staff is noteworthy.

PRO ref: MUN 5/394

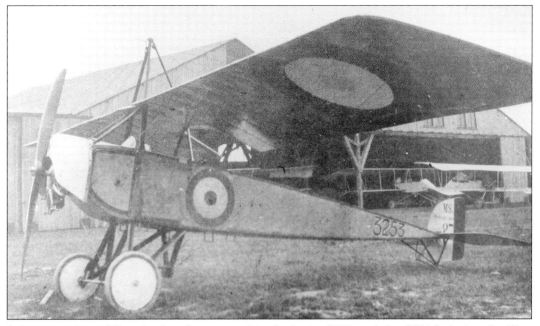

A large number of French aircraft were used by both the RFC and the RNAS during the First World War. Much fine work was carried out in these machines, but none could claim greater fame than the Morane-Saulnier MS 3 Type L. Twenty-five were delivered to the RNAS, where they were generally known as the Morane Parasol. While out on what was intended as a routine bombing mission, 3253 won undying fame in the hands of Flight Sub-Lieutenant R.A.J. Warneford of 1 Wing RNAS, when he managed to climb his 80 h.p. machine above Zeppelin LZ 37 over Ghent and bomb it on 7 June 1915. This was the first Zeppelin to be destroyed in the air. Warneford received the first RNAS VC, and only the second to be awarded to an airman.

FAAM ref: MORANE SAULNIER/3

Many Nieuports were also used; not only single-seat scouts, but also the Type 12, a small two-seater with a wingspan of less than 30 ft. Unusually, no rear gun is visible on this machine from 1 Wing RNAS, operating from Dunkirk at the turn of 1915/16. This is a French-built example; British-built machines differed in having circular cowlings.

FAAM ref: N/PORT 18

HMS *Campania* (18,000 tons), was converted from an old twenty-three knot Cunard liner, having been purchased cheaply from ship-breakers. Aircraft took off from the ship's 245 ft sloping flight deck, but could not land on it. She was credited with being able to carry ten or eleven aircraft, including Short 184s, and had stowage for eight 14-in air-launched torpedoes. She is seen here just out of the Cammell Laird yard on 5 April 1916, shortly after a post-refit recommissioning.

PRO ref: ADM 176/884

The single-engined SS (Submarine Scout) series of non-rigid airships were the first in widespread use, entering service in 1915. They were relatively small at 143 ft long with a volume of only 60–70,000 cubic ft. This is one of only twelve, with cars based on Maurice Farman aircraft nacelles. Although top speed was a meagre 40 m.p.h. and bomb load only some 250 lbs, they achieved their object of keeping the enemy's head down. British non-rigid airships were far more successful than the later, larger and better-known rigids. The nose contours were maintained by an aluminium cone and radiating stiff canes. This example is seen at its mooring mast at Barrow. It appears that its gas bags are being topped-up.

PRO ref: AIR 11/241

The Coastals were probably the most successful class of non-rigid airships. Twenty-seven of these were built for the Royal Naval Air Service. They were 196 ft long, with a volume of 170,000 cubic ft. Anti-submarine bombs (four × 100 lb or two × 230 lb) and two machine guns were carried and maximum endurance was about twenty-four hours. This is C.9, which logged more service flying hours than any other British airship – 2,500 in total – and had an outstanding career, with the greatest number of recorded actions against the enemy. At 0615 on 23 July 1916, and commanded by Flight Sub-Lieutenant J.G. Struthers, C.9 joined the destroyer HMS *Foyle* in a sweep of the Western Approaches. It was fired on by British troops in Jersey, although the resultant loss of gas was not realized at the time. Engine trouble was experienced and the ship came down near the destroyer at 0105 next morning. *Foyle* towed C.9, now partly deflated and collapsed, to Mullion Cove. Weather conditions caused C.9 first to rise and then to strike the sea, causing damage and the crew were taken off. On reaching Mullion, C.9 was walked inland and successfully deflated. It was later returned to service.

PRO ref: ADM 131/64

This photograph shows Short 184 No. 8075 on board the seaplane carrier HM Fleet Auxiliary *Anne*, the new name given to HMS *Aenne Rickmers* on 5 August 1915. The date is probably post-1915, as there is no Union Flag painted on the fuselage.

FAAM ref: SHORT/306

It was decided to fit 2-pounder guns to the new Class 23 and 23X rigid airships, and it therefore became important to ensure that firing the gun would not endanger the airship itself. Tests were carried out to check whether the muzzle flash would ignite a representational dummy. Here the gun is being fired into a hydrogen-filled gas bag. The tests were successful, as no ignition took place. The gun was later fitted to ship No. 23, but the scheme was abandoned when the Class 23 craft proved to be severely overweight.

PRO ref: AIR 1/2589

The seaplane carrier HMS *Vindex* was converted from the Isle of Man ferry *Viking* of 2,950 tons. She was three knots slower than *Campania* and had a short (65 ft) flying-off deck and small hangar forward for fighters only. The hangar aft, fitted with two electric handling cranes, could accommodate one small and four large floatplanes.

PRO ref: ADM 176/1125

Naval Airship No. 9 (R.9) was a rigid ship, 526 ft long and with a volume of 846,000 cubic ft. It was an unsuccessful design, used mainly for training, and flew only 198 hours. This photograph was taken at the Naval Airship Station Walney Island, Barrow, on 25 October 1916. No. 15 gas bag has been deflated and removed while the ship is suspended from the shed roof. The figure at the lower right gives the scale.

PRO ref: AIR 1/2654
CN 5/16

The seaplane carrier HMS *Raven II* of 4,678 tons was converted from the German prize *Rabenfels*, and is seen here moored in Castelorizo Harbour. The idyllic surroundings are deceptive, as the enemy coast is clearly visible, and it was here that the Turks shelled the *Ben-my-Chree*. The date is probably 1915–16.

FAAM ref: CARS R/47

On the night of 25–26 January 1917 the seaplane carriers HMS *Ben-my-Chree* and *Raven II* left Port Said to mount an attack on Turkish communications. Four aircraft were launched; Short 184 No. 8080, Sopwith Schneiders Nos. 3770 and 3778, and Sopwith Baby No. 8188, all carrying 65 lb bombs. Led by Wing Commander C.R. Samson, they attacked a bridge across the Irmak river at Chilkaldere, some eighteen miles east of Adana, which carried the Baghdad railway. Samson attacked from low level and his bomb scored a direct hit.

PRO ref: ADM 116/1353

Flight Sub-Lieutenant A.W. Clemson then hit the target with two bombs, but all these missiles were too light to destroy the bridge. However, it was sufficiently weakened to disrupt traffic.

PRO ref: ADM 116/1353

In one of many operations against Turkish forces, a miscellany of naval aircraft from Thasos Air Station attacked the seaplane base at Gereviz on 27 February 1917. Four Henri Farmans, two Sopwith 'bombers', a Sopwith 'fighter' and a Bristol Scout took part. As well as two possible hits on a hangar with 65 lb bombs, an Albatros W1 (arrowed on the shore line, top right) was forced down and strafed. At least one Rumpler 6B 1 in German markings and another Albatros are also visible.

PRO ref: ADM 116/1353

The superlative Sopwith Triplane was a major trend-setter, inspiring a series of similar machines which included the famous Fokker Dr 1. The fast-climbing Sopwith outclassed the previously-feared Albatros D III and gained a reputation which belied the fact that only 140 were delivered. These are 1 Squadron RNAS machines at Furnes, Belgium, in early 1917; '15 Peggy' is N5387 and '16' is N5425.

FAAM ref: S/WITH T/PLANE 17

Because they were unable to take off from the water in rough weather, ways of enabling float planes to take off from carriers were sought. A split-tube guide rail was installed along the flight deck of HMS *Campania*, allowing a float plane to take off by means of a 12 ft long four-wheeled trolley axle beneath its floats. Stops at the bow detached the axle at the end of the take-off run. Here, Flight Sub-Lieutenant A.R.T. Pipon takes off successfully on 16 April 1917 in Short 184 No. 8028 after a run of some 170 ft, having reached 24 knots along the ramp, with *Campania* herself making 17 knots, and despite the trolley having skipped over the port-side stop.

PRO ref: AIR 1/636/17/122/129

CN 5/17

There was concern in the Grand Fleet that marauding Zeppelins would report its movements and thus enable the German High Seas Fleet to avoid battle. One way of countering this perceived menace was to carry fighters on capital ships and cruisers. Here, a Sopwith Scout, better known by its colloquial name of 'Pup' is leaving a turret-top ramp. This may well be N6453 being flown off B turret of the battlecruiser HMS *Repulse* on 1 October 1917 by Squadron Commander F.J. Rutland.

PRO ref: AIR 1/720/35/19

The most famous of the early aircraft-carrying ships was undoubtedly HMS *Furious* (19,100 tons), which was commissioned on 26 June 1917 and went on to survive the Second World War, having served with great distinction. She was never fitted with the forward 18-in gun, but the Elswick yard, where this photograph was taken in 1917, fitted her with a hangar for eight aircraft and flying-off

deck forward. Her continuous high speed of 30 knots made her a valuable asset, but the single monster gun aft was, of course, virtually useless.

PRO ref: ADM 176/283

This undated view of the famous seaplane base at Royal Naval Air Station Calshot reveals a wealth of interesting details. On the far left is a Twin Blackburn; towards the centre is an aircraft graveyard; while between the hangars are folded floatplanes and a flying boat hull. At the top is what appears to be a large flying boat, close to which a floatplane (probably Short 184) rides off-shore.

PRO ref: AIR 29/8

This impressive German flying boat is the sole Dornier (Zeppelin-Lindau) Rs II, which was originally built in mid-1916 with three engines but later modified to a four-engined layout. It was rebuilt again after an accident, the tailplane being heavily modified, and is seen here in that condition in the late summer of 1917. This unique machine weighed 9,158 kgs and had a 33.2 m wingspan. The crude retouching, including the Patée cross on the port fin, is on the original print.

PRO ref: AIR 1/716/27/19/29

The Felixstowe flying boats were remarkably successful and seaworthy machines. Spanning 102 ft, the F3 was larger than the better-known F2A. It also had a longer range and twice the bomb load, although it was not so manoeuvrable. Both aircrew and ground crew are included in this clear but damaged photograph of N4258 on its beaching trolley. The startling paint scheme was designed to enable the aircraft to be spotted easily if it force-landed on the sea. Many F3s, which served with RNAS and, later, RAF squadrons around the UK and the Mediterranean, had enclosed cockpits.

FAAM ref: FELIXSTOWE/65

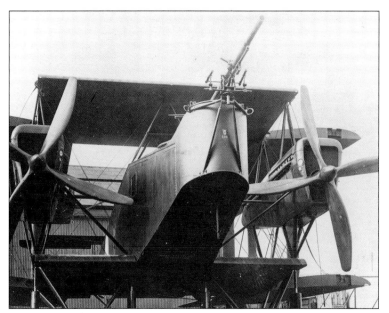

The use of large bombers was pioneered by the far-sighted RNAS. The first true heavy bomber was the Handley Page 0/100 which had a wingspan of 100 ft and was nicknamed the 'Bloody Paralyser'. This example is No. 3127 of 14 Squadron, based at Redcar during September 1917 for anti-submarine operations. The coaming of the front gunner's cockpit has been raised by 8 in and a 6-pounder Davis recoilless gun experimentally fitted.

FAAM ref: HANDLEY PAGE/38

During both World Wars the women of the Royal Navy, including its air arm, provided an indispensable but underplayed contribution to victory. These members of the Women's Royal Naval Service are helping with flight deck training 'somewhere in Britain', probably towards the end of the war. The fighter is a Bristol Scout D, N540? The cut-out in the centre section is evidence of a machine-gun having been carried at some time. The three-bay aircraft in the background could be a Sopwith Cuckoo or Wight Bomber.

FAAM air: PERSONNEL/1645

Short 184 No. 9055 from the seaplane carrier HMS *Manxman* was photographed over Brindisi while flying at 1,000 ft on 2 January 1918.

PRO ref: AIR 2/37

Hoisting Short 184 No. 8033 on board *Manxman* at Brindisi on 11 January 1918. The rails are for manoeuvring the aircraft on their trolleys. The Short 184 was the most important British naval aircraft of the First World War equating to the later Fairey Swordfish. Over 650 were built. Its greatest claim to fame was the first-ever sinking of an enemy ship by torpedo attack.

PRO ref: AIR 2/37

A rare sight. Three famous seaplane carriers together. HMS *Ark Royal* (1914) has caught the sun; *Manxman* an ex-Isle of Man ferry of 3,091 tons, lies off to port, while ahead of her, with a floatplane in the water, is HMS *Empress*, converted from a channel packet of 2,510 tons. They were photographed from 1,000 ft off Mudros on 30 January 1918.

PRO ref: AIR 2/37

The Short 320, the manufacturer's type number equating to the power of its Sunbeam Cossack engine, was designed to carry the new Mk.IX 18-in torpedo weighing 1,000 lbs. However, opportunities to use it for planned set-piece attacks on Central Powers fleets at Wilmhelmshaven and Pola were missed. This machine, N1155, was part of *Manxman*'s complement at Mudros on 30 January 1918.

PRO ref: AIR 2/37

Although the Sopwith 1½–Strutter, known in the RNAS as the Type 9700, is best known as a two-seater fighter, a large number were modified as single-seat bombers, with internal racks for four 65 lb bombs. N5520 C3 is such a machine and may have belonged to a training unit, as it has no Vickers gun in this early 1918 view.

FAAM ref: SOPWITH 1½/30

The Sopwith Cuckoo was the first successful landplane torpedo-carrier; the delivery vehicle in the world's first 'weapons system'. This is N.74, the prototype. Originally serialled simply T for torpedo-plane, it first flew in July 1917. The prototype's 200 h.p. Hispano-Suiza engine was changed to the less reliable Sunbeam Arab on production machines and, as late as 29 May 1918, it was remarked that trials were being delayed by engine trouble. However, the file contains the prophetic words '. . . here we have a weapon of great potential'. The torpedo is the 1,000 lb Mk.IX.

PRO ref: AIR 1/643/17/122/257

Frequently encountered by British units, the Friedrichshafen FF49C reconnaissance and air sea rescue floatplane was extremely seaworthy and highly regarded. No. 1796, from Sylt, was forced down on 19 June 1918. It shows no sign of serious damage and the crew appear unhurt. Equipped with a radio receiver and transmitter, it was armed with a Parabellum machine-gun on a ring mounting for the observer.

PRO ref: ADM 137/1954

In addition to flying aircraft off turret-top platforms on large warships, fighters were towed on lighters behind destroyers to extend their radius of action. By 1918, Sopwith Camels did actually take off from the lighters to intercept prowling Zeppelins. This photograph of N6812, a Bentley-powered 2F1, was taken on 17 July 1918 during pre-flight trials.

PRO ref: AIR 1/643/17/122/274

| | |
|---|---|
| Axle Clamp Pin. | A. |
| Releasing Wire. | B. |
| Front Securing Wires. | C. & D. |
| Standing Rear Wheel Chock. | E. |
| Tail Guide Trestle. | F. |
| Tail Securing Wires. | H. |
| Front Wheel Moveable Chocks. | J.J. |
| Axle Clamp. | K. |

This is a standard 56 ft hydroplane lighter for launching Camels. The take-off ramps which sloped down from stern to bow, widened forward to allow for the aircraft swinging on take off. For the first such take-off, on 31 July 1918, the lighter was towed at 32 knots by the destroyer HMS *Truculent*. Identification roundels have been painted on both sides, and there is evidence that the whole deck is camouflaged.

PRO ref: AIR 1/643/17/122/260

The Hansa-Brandenburg W12 two-seat floatplane fighter was a feared and respected opponent of British aircraft and small ships. This example was forced down in September 1918. It is aircraft No. 2119 from the sixth batch, with three guns, cockpit doors and connecting struts between the ailerons. The prancing horse staffel marking is noteworthy.

PRO ref: ADM 137/1954

Although this could almost be a scene from the Battle of the Atlantic, the dazzle-painted merchant ships are typical of the so-called Great War. This is part of convoy HG 102 from Gibraltar to the East Coast, photographed by an escorting aircraft from Bembridge, probably a Short 184, while passing up the English Channel on 6 September 1918.

PRO ref: ADM 137/2771

To counter rumoured fast new German commerce raiders, five large light cruisers of the 'Elizabethan' class were laid down, armed with seven × 7.5-in guns. Only one saw service in the First World War, and then as a small aircraft carrier of 9,394 tons. Three of her heavy guns were removed and a hangar and separate landing-on and flying-off decks fitted. Originally named HMS *Cavendish*, she was renamed *Vindictive* in honour of the heroine of the 1918 Zeebrugge raid. Her high speed of 30 knots permitted her, together with the larger *Furious*, to operate as a scout for the battle fleet.

PRO ref: ADM 176/1126

# FROM WORLD LEADERSHIP TO LEAN DECADES

The Parnall Panther was among the earliest aircraft designed to operate from carriers. A two-seat spotter-reconnaissance machine, it incorporated a hydrovane, to prevent nosing over in the event of a ditching, together with flotation bags. It shared built-in ugliness with several other early British shipboard aircraft.

PRO ref: AIR 1/728/176/3/38

The original caption to this photograph reads 'Towing Panther at D-B'. Except that this is N95, the fifth prototype, nothing else is known, but D-B could be Donibristle. The Panther, some of which went to the Japanese and US Navies, was unusual in having a folding monocoque fuselage.

PRO ref: AIR 1/728/176/3/38

The N.S. (North Sea) twin-engined airships which entered service in 1917 were much larger than any of their operational predecessors, having a length of 260 ft and a volume of 360,000 cubic ft. N.S. 11 was one of the most famous of the British non-rigid airships. It set a number of records, including an endurance marathon of 100 hours 50 minutes in February 1919, under the Command of Group Captain W.K.J. Warneford. Tragically, it was destroyed on 15 July, exploding after being struck by lightning off the Norfolk coast.

PRO ref: AIR 11/241

The first Cuckoos embarked in HMS *Argus* on 19 October 1918, but the war ended before they could be deployed. Here, Cuckoos from the Development Flight at RNAS Gosport are making a formation practice attack on fleet units in Portland Harbour on 29 July 1919. The unit became 210 Squadron in 1920.

FAAM ref: ARMS/BOMBS/54

Under the direction of John Porte, the Seaplane Experimental Station at Felixstowe designed the finest fighting flying boats of the First World War for the RNAS; many being improved versions of US Curtiss machines. The large Porte Baby, the renowned F2A and the officially-inspired F3 led to the huge Fury, or Porte Flying Super Boat of 1918; a 100 per cent British triplane of 123 ft span and powered by five Rolls-Royce Eagle engines, delivering a total of 1,750 h.p. Like the Handley Page V/1500 four-engined bomber, the Fury was too large and expensive for the post-war services. It is seen here in its final configuration at RAF Felixstowe on 11 August 1919. It was successfully flown at up to 33,000 lbs weight.

PRO ref: AIR 1/716/27/19/29

In the aftermath of the Bolshevik revolution British forces supported the White Russians. Among the aircraft used by the naval element of the North Russian Expeditionary Force were Fairey IIIC bomber-reconnaissance aircraft, another of the new post-war types. These were taken to Russia on board HMS *Pegasus* (2,070 tons), converted from the mercantile *Stockholm*. Floatplanes were based at Murmansk and at Archangel, on the River Dvina. At the seaplane beach at Troitsa on the Dvina, with an encampment in the background, aircraft of the Archangel River Seaplane Squadron are being prepared for the day's work. Fairey IIIC N9242, one of a batch converted from Type IIIB especially for the North Russian Expedition, bombed-up with two × 112 lb, is setting off.

PRO ref: AIR 1/10/15/1/35
CN 5/25/34

Northern Russia again, with Fairey IIIC floatplanes on seaplane lighters. This was a cheap and simple method of local transport, which was nevertheless unpopular because getting the aircraft waterborne took longer than from the beached positions and raised the risk of damaged floats. The stillness of the water is remarkable.

PRO ref: AIR 1/10/15/1/35
CN 5/25/35

A Fairey IIIC has come to grief, apparently without too much damage, and a floating crane is standing by to pick up the casualty. Even without such mishaps, the aircraft of the ARS Squadron suffered from fabric affected by the local damp conditions providing poor lift which limited bomb loads.

PRO ref: AIR 1/10/15/1/35
CN 5/25/36

Short 184 N9261 is up on its floats and about to take off into Russian skies.

PRO ref: AIR 1/10/15/1/35

CN 5/25/39

HMS *Argus*, 14,450 tons, was converted from the incomplete Italian liner *Conte Rosso* and clearly shows both her original lines and the modifications made to convert her into an aircraft carrier. She was the first with a full-length flush flight deck and could carry twenty aircraft. Prominent features include a retractable charthouse, radio aerials and massive cranes to bring seaplanes on board under the flight deck aft. She entered service in September 1918, painted in dazzle camouflage. This appears to be an early post-war view. The aircraft on deck is a Sopwith Camel fitted with a hydrovane to prevent it from nosing over on ditching.

PRO ref: ADM 176/42

The 'S' class destroyer HMS *Stronghold* was involved in the experimental flying-off of aircraft from a simple counter-weight catapult on her bows. Two light aircraft could be carried; one on a platform aft of the launching rails and the other before the bridge in place of No. 1 gun. This photograph, probably taken in early 1925, shows one of the tiny 22 ft span Royal Aircraft Factory 'Aerial Target' aircraft. The designation was deliberately misleading, as the aircraft were in fact radio-controlled flying bombs, fitted with 30 h.p. ABC Gnat engines. The file reveals official dismay over indiscreet press coverage.

PRO ref: ADM 1/8676/47

CN 1/4

This is a later picture of **HMS** *Vindictive*, see page 34. She has been reconverted to a cruiser, with only No. 2 gun missing, still displaced by the small hangar for up to six seaplanes. Most significant is the catapult, powered by compressed air and the first to be fitted to a British cruiser. The first catapult launches took place in 1925 and paved the way for aircraft at sea on most major units of the fleet, thereby greatly extending surveillance ranges in pre-radar days. The large crane was a necessary adjunct for handling seaplanes.

PRO ref: ADM 176/1126

Piracy remained a serious problem in Chinese waters during the 1920s and 30s. Here, HMS *Argus* (1918) and *Hermes* (1924), the first ship designed from the keel up as an aircraft carrier, are seen from a Fairey IIID out of Kai Tak at 1317 on 1 September 1927 off Fan Lo Kong. Pirate junks were attacked by IIIDs from *Hermes* in Bias Bay, near Tsang Chau. A landing party under Captain L.D.J. Mackinnon RN then went ashore to destroy junks, sampans, pirate houses and the brothel areas. Whole villages were not destroyed.

PRO ref: ADM 116/2502

Fairey Flycatcher N9965 of 401 Flight in the hands of maintenance staff at Royal Naval Air Station Kai Tak, the airfield serving HMS *Tamar*, Hong Kong, during 1927. The Flycatcher was the standard Fleet fighter from 1923 to 1934.

FAAM ref: F/CATCHER 140

HMS *Vindictive* carried Fairey IIID spotter-reconnaissance floatplanes of 444 Flight during the 1920s. N9469 is seen ashore at Wei-hai-wei, China, in about 1927. The variety of clothing is interesting.

FAAM ref: FAIREY/265

The Blackburn Dart was the Royal Navy's next torpedo carrier. It entered service with 460 and 461 Flights in 1923 and served until 1933. With 450 h.p. available, the Dart was intended to use the 18-in Mk.VIII torpedo, originally a submarine weapon, which weighed some 1,400 lbs and had a large enough warhead to seriously damage a warship. Shown here is 460 Flight aboard HMS *Eagle* in the Mediterranean in about 1928. Identifiable machines include N9823 '60', N9819 '62' and N9692 '67'. Their fuselage bands, on which the fleet numbers are marked, are in the *Eagle*'s colour, black. The torpedoes carried here are the lighter Mk.IX. The Dart was a more potent weapon than the big-gun admirals of the era realised – or admitted.

FAAM ref: DART/16

HMS *Albatross*, a 4,800 ton seaplane carrier, was built for the Royal Australian Navy. She was the last British example of the type. Her aircraft complement comprised Supermarine Seagull Mk.III amphibians: this is A9–7 in about 1929. She was later purchased for the Royal Navy and re-commissioned on 31 July 1939.

PRO ref: ADM 176/799

This is the result of the major reconstruction of HMS *Courageous*, one of the three light battlecruisers or large light cruisers known as 'Fisher's Follies'. She recommissioned as a fleet carrier on 14 February 1928. Aircraft capacity was a useful forty-eight. Bulges have been added to improve stability, affected by the greatly-increased top weight. She, together with the similarly-treated *Glorious* and *Furious*, had become world-class fleet carriers. Of the three, only *Furious* lacked the starboard deck-edge island. There were aircraft-handling cranes at both ends of the hangar and palisades and wires aft of the island to prevent aircraft without arrester gear from going over the side. Fighters could take off directly from the hangar along the sloping lower flight deck, often referred to as a slip deck.

PRO ref: ADM 176/163

On the afternoon of 1 April 1931 HMS *Glorious* (23,250 tons), converted from a light battlecruiser, was conducting flying operations east of Gibraltar. She entered thick fog shortly afterwards and turned back to clear it and recover aircraft. However, this course was soon reversed because of the risk of collision with her consorts. A ship's siren was heard and *Glorious* went to Emergency Full Astern, but way was still on and she struck the French liner *Florida* of 9,331 grt. *Florida* was carrying 691 passengers and crew, and was hit on the port bow at just after 1629 as she tried to turn away to starboard.

PRO ref: ADM 116/2876

*Glorious* cut a wide gash some 62 ft deep in *Florida*'s side, resulting in the death of twenty-four passengers and crew. One seaman was killed on *Glorious*, which suffered the destruction of the bow over a length of some 60 ft from the lower flying-off deck to above the keel. The incident caused four Flycatcher fighters to run out of fuel and ditch. The *Florida* was towed stern-first to Malaga by the destroyers HMS *Verity* and *Wryneck*, accompanied by *Glorious*, which had taken off survivors. *Glorious* was given a temporary bow before proceeding to Malta for more permanent repairs.

PRO ref: ADM 116/2876

The Hawker Nimrod Mk.I, so streamlined compared with the earlier Flycatcher, was the naval version of the RAF's elegant Fury single-seat fighter. This particular machine, S1583, is '576' of 408 Flight from HMS *Glorious*, seen over the Mediterranean in 1931. The fuselage band is yellow. It met its end on 5 February 1932, when it overran the flight deck and crashed onto the slip deck below; Lieutenant J.P.G. Bryant RN escaped unhurt.

FAAM ref: NIMROD/50

The successor to the Dart was the Blackburn Ripon, which became the Fleet Air Arm's first landplane torpedo-bomber, i.e. the first which could undertake horizontal bombing duties with the benefit of a bomb-aimer. These red-banded examples are aircraft of 465 Flight from HMS *Furious* in the winter of 1931–2. The six aircraft are Mk.IIAs identified as S1566 '7', S1558 '9', S1561 '8', S1565 '4', S1554 '5' and S1555 '6'.

FAAM ref: RIPON/50

Deck landing has always been a hazardous undertaking, although since the mid-1950s the British-invented angled deck and mirror (projector) sight dramatically decreased the risks involved. While conducting flying operations off Wei-hai-wei on 22 June 1932, HMS *Hermes* lost Fairey IIIF Mk.IIIB S1477, probably of 440 Flight. Captain R.M. Giddy RM has landed port wing low and is heading for the edge of the flight deck. The observer, Lieutenant Commander E.R. Dymott, is already alert and up in his cockpit.

PRO ref: ADM 116/2844

Fortunately, the crew were saved, although the aircraft sank. The plane-guard destroyer, not needed on this occasion, is bearing down on the carrier's port quarter.

PRO ref: ADM 116/2844

HMS *Eagle* was converted from the incomplete Chilean super-dreadnought *Almirante Cochrane*, weighing in at 22,600 tons in 1920. She could originally accommodate twenty-one aircraft, and was unique among fleet carriers in having two conventional funnels. In this 1933 photograph she carries her interim pre-war armament of single 6-in, 4.7 in and 2-pounder (40 mm pom-pom)

guns, together with an octuple 2-pounder mounting between her funnels. She is painted in China Station colours of white hull and buff upperworks.

PRO ref: ADM 176/221

Chinese pirates raided the SS *Shuntien*, taking hostages, in position 38.10N 118.10E. A punitive mission was planned and a searching Fairey IIIF coded '81' of 824 Squadron from HMS *Eagle*, flown by Lieutenant Commander A.M. Randle, located the pirate junks on 20 June 1934. The junks fired on Randle's aircraft.

PRO ref: ADM 116/3253

The Hawker Osprey Mk.I two-seat fighter-reconnaissance aircraft was a development of the Hart light bomber. These 803 Squadron machines were ranged on *Eagle* in anticipation of an attack on the pirate stronghold, but were not needed. The chequer-finned '291', with the 'eyebrows', is K2783 and '294' is S1689.

FAAM ref: OSPREY/80

Hostages Mr Sun Tan Ling and Mr Nicholl being brought back safely by Lieutenant D.Mc. J. Russell RN in Fairey IIIF Mk.IIIB spotter-reconnaissance floatplane S1474 '74' . . .

PRO ref: ADM 116/3253

. . . and by Lieutenant D.C.V. Pelly RN in Mk.IIIB S1821 '83' respectively at 1310 on 20 June 1934.

PRO ref: ADM 116/3253

The Blackburn Baffin was basically the Ripon re-engined with the air-cooled Bristol Pegasus radial, which was lighter than the latter's liquid-cooled Napier Lion. It entered service in 1934. This is 810 Squadron, ashore at RAF North Coates Fitties armament camp, Lincolnshire, in July 1935. The nearest machine is S1665, converted from a Ripon, and coded '02' on the blue band of

the parent carrier HMS *Courageous*. The contemporary mix of RN and RAF personnel is a clear
reminder that the aircraft belonged to the Fleet Air Arm of the Royal Air Force at that time.

FAAM ref: BAFFIN/47

After repairs and a refit, *Glorious* emerged with her quarterdeck raised, flight deck extended right
aft and, invisible in this view, two accelerators (catapults) fitted at the forward end of the flight deck.
Octuple pom-poms have been fitted aft of the island and on the lower flying-off deck.

PRO ref: ADM 176/296

Blackburn Shark Mk.I torpedo-spotter-reconnaissance aircraft K4350 is '647' of 820 Squadron, based on HMS *Courageous*. In 1935 it was loaned to the Torpedo Development Unit at Gosport, for the testing of a new torpedo rack to carry a Mk.VIII* torpedo, $2\frac{1}{2}°$ nose down. The results were not satisfactory, TDU recommending that $4\frac{1}{2}°$ would be better. The Shark was an early example of a multi-rôle combat aircraft.

PRO ref: AVIA 16/12

Succeeding the IIIF was the Fairey Seal, which, as a bomber-spotter-reconnaissance landplane, was another early multi-rôle combat aircraft. This 1935–6 view shows K3515 from 823 Squadron on HMS *Glorious*, which can be seen below the starboard wing tip. It wears its Fleet Number '812' on a yellow band.

FAAM ref: F SEAL/34

These colourful Nimrods and Ospreys from 800 Squadron wear the blue markings of *Courageous*, and are seen in about May 1937. Osprey K5756 '123' is believed to be the CO's personal aircraft. The other machines are: Ospreys K5753 '124' and K5744 '125'; and Nimrods S1615 '102', S1631 '103', K2829 '104', S1628(?) '105', K2840 '107', S1584 '109' and K2838 '120'.

FAAM ref: NIM/21

Catapult seaplanes were literally the eyes of the fleet in the 1930s and early 1940s. HMS *Exeter*, a small heavy cruiser of 8,390 tons, was equipped with two catapults and two Supermarine Walrus Mk.I amphibious flying boats: K8340 '769' and K8557 '780', both of 718 Squadron. Part of the 8th Cruiser Squadron, she wears light grey paint for duty in the West Indies. Despite the label on the original print, the date could not have been earlier than May 1937, which is when K8557 first flew.

PRO ref: ADM 176/248

There was a substantial Royal Naval presence at Singapore on 14 February 1938 for the official opening of the King George VI Graving Dock, seen at bottom right, by His Excellency the Governor of the Straits Settlements. HMS *Eagle* was the largest ship present. She had three union flags (one is under the large marquee) painted on the flight deck as neutrality markings during the Sino–Japanese war. A stream of cars is arriving and many spectators are already in place.

PRO ref: ADM 116/3664

HMS *Hermes*, of 10,850 tons, is seen here in August 1938. She was too small to be fully effective, her capacity for even early aircraft being only fifteen, and the useable length of her flight deck was substantially reduced by a long round-down aft. The huge control top would not have looked out of place on a battleship.

PRO ref: ADM 176/331

# BLOOD, TOIL, SWEAT AND TRIUMPH

Blackburn Shark Mk.III K8901, here in full war paint, served as '24' with the Torpedo Training Unit at Gosport in January and February 1940, then moved north with the unit to Abbotsinch. The Shark was a relatively advanced biplane, with a twin-row engine and W-truss wing bracing in place of the usual struts and wires.

FAAM ref: SHARK/50

Blackburn Rocs bound for Finland, but did they go? Despite undoubtedly good intentions, to have actually supplied these inadequate fighters could have been construed as aiding Finland's Russian enemies. The location is Dyce and the date is March 1940. There is activity around these Finnish Rocs, and at least two have their engines running. A total of thirty three were allocated to Finland as RO-141 to RO-173. Among those in the group are RO-141 and RO-143. All lack the blue Finnish swastika on the white disc, although in another view of the same scene RO-150 has one crudely marked.

FAAM ref: ROC/39

This photograph was taken by Petty Officer Hart, Telegraphist Air Gunner in Blackburn Skua Mk.II dive-bomber L2908 '6K' of 800 Squadron, during the disastrous attack on the battlecruiser *Scharnhorst* (34,851 tons, nine × 28-cm guns) in Trondheim harbour on 13 June 1940. The pilot was Lieutenant K.V. Spurway RN. Eight out of the fifteen Skuas, which had flown from HMS *Ark Royal* were lost, and only one hit with a 500 lb bomb was obtained. Some of the Skuas were seen to attack the heavy cruiser *Admiral Hipper*. The aircraft which escaped were mainly those which stayed low after their dives. Flak of all calibres from shore batteries and the assembled warships would have been formidable. Also, many German fighters were present, alerted by a badly-planned but well-executed RAF attack on Vaernes aerodrome.

PRO ref: ADM 199/480

In response to Italy's declaration of war, the FAA training unit at La Polyvestre airfield at Hyères in southern France became operational, although it initially retained its second-line identity as 767 Squadron. Bombing raids were immediately flown against targets on the Italian mainland. Fairey Swordfish Mk.I K8427, coded 'TOV' and loaded with three French 250 kg bombs, was one of nine aircraft to attack targets in the Genoa area on 19 June 1940. The most famous of all British naval aircraft, the Swordfish filled the TSR rôle.

FAAM ref: SWFH/525

When their carriers were not available, shore-based Skuas made many attacks on German installations from France to Norway. Here, an 801 Squadron aircraft from RNAS Hatston is seen over Reksteren, Norway, on 1 August 1940. On these long sorties the Skuas carried a limited bomb load of one × 250 lb and four × 20 lb, as seen here. The Skua won undying fame by sinking the *Königsberg*.

PRO ref: ADM 199/450

CN 1/38/102

804 Squadron flew Gloster Sea Gladiators throughout most of 1940. N2272 is a Sea Gladiator (Interim), converted from an RAF Gladiator Mk.II. Uncoded, it bears a striking personal emblem, featuring a fist in a pilot's uniform punching through an Italian *fasces* into a swastika. In the cockpit is Lieutenant J. Sleigh RN, and standing, left to right, are Sub-Lieutenant Balme, Sub-Lieutenant (A) B. Paterson and Sub-Lieutenant N.H. Patterson. The period is September 1940.

PRO ref: ADM 207/8

Skuas of 801 Squadron from Hatston struck targets at Haugesund on 3 October 1940. However, records suggest that the large freighter under attack was not significantly damaged.

PRO ref: ADM 199/450

CN 1/38/36

While at Hatston, 804 Squadron was re-equipped with the US Grumman Martlet Mk.1, the FAA's first single-seat monoplane, before moving across the island to Skeabrae. Sub-Lieutenant (A) D. Hutchinson went off the runway at Skeabrae and tipped over at the end of his landing run on 17 November 1940, but 'S7B' (serial number unknown) was soon repaired. The Martlet Is were ex-French machines with non-folding wings; this and other problems prevented them from being embarked operationally.

PRO ref: ADM 207/8

(*Opposite, bottom*) Each fleet carrier included between two and six of the heavy and impressive Mk.V or Mk.VI octuple 2-pounder water-cooled Vickers pom-poms. However, their bark was worse than their bite, as low muzzle velocity and relatively short range meant that the huge quantities of ammunition pumped into the sky (720–920 rounds per minute, per mounting) often failed to actually hit anything. This mounting is on board HMS *Illustrious* early in her career.

PRO ref: INF 2/45 pt.1

Rocs on board carriers were a rarity. This unidentified target tug has met with a minor accident on board HMS *Formidable* (23,000 tons) during her work-up at Scapa Flow in early December 1940.

FAAM ref: ROC/48

A month before formal commissioning, the new 'Illustrious' class fleet carrier HMS *Victorious* (23,000 tons) was photographed on 16 April 1941, during her acceptance trials, by a Blenheim of 608 Squadron RAF. Her elaborate camouflage extends to the flight deck. The first three armoured carriers could originally accommodate only thirty-six aircraft, including three dismantled spares.

PRO ref: AIR 28/828

The Deck Landing Control Officer or batsman on *Illustrious* is giving a 'Roger' (aircraft is OK for height and line-up) to the pilot of a Grumman Martlet. DLCOs were responsible for safe landing procedures by giving visual instructions to pilots.

PRO ref: INF 2/45 pt 1

The finale of the Blackburn Skua's operational career with 800 Squadron, the FAA's premier unit, was enacted as the aircraft prepared to leave *Ark Royal* (1938) for the last time en route for England, in April 1941.

FAAM ref: SKUA/63

During operations against the pro-Axis regime in Iraq, Swordfish of 814 Squadron were disembarked from *Hermes* and based at RAF Shaibah. There the only bombs available were of First World War pattern. On 14 May the barracks at Amara were attacked by 814 Squadron, using ancient 520 lb bombs which are seen bursting on the target.

PRO ref: ADM 199/1096

Not what it seems. In the early years of the war, the Royal Navy repeated the First World War subterfuge of converting merchant ships to resemble major warships. During the Spring of 1940, Force W was formed at Scapa Flow from two dummy 'R' class battleships and a dummy of the carrier HMS *Hermes*. The latter was in fact the 477½ ft long SS *Mamari* of 7,924 grt, which was given a mock flight deck and superstructure supported on wooden uprights. The realistic conversion, which was known as Fleet Tender C, and unarmed except for one Lewis gun, was intended to deceive the enemy and to attract Luftwaffe bombers from real targets. She is seen here on 30 August 1940, photographed by a Hudson of 224 Squadron RAF.

PRO ref: AIR 28/471

A routine deployment on 1 June 1941 found Fleet Tender C, the pretend *Hermes*, joining a convoy of slow coasters sailing south along the East Coast from Scotland. Next day she ran onto the wreck of the tanker *Ahamo* in the shallow waters of the Wold Channel off Norfolk, stuck fast and sank. On 3 June the wreck was torpedoed by German S-boats, but was not finally demolished until 1949. The wreck of '*Hermes*' is seen here on 21 October 1941.

PRO ref: AIR 28/595

On 6 June 1941, Swordfish from *Eagle* bombed and sank the German blockade runner *Elbe* of 9,179 grt in mid-Atlantic, while she was masquerading as the *Kristiania Fjord*.

PRO ref: ADM 199/809

The armoured fleet carrier *Victorious*, carrying several radar arrays, has Fairey Fulmar eight-gun two-seat fighters on deck (one with its tail up and ready for catapulting) in about mid-1941. She survived the war and was successfully rebuilt and modernized at Portsmouth in the 1950s.

PRO ref: ADM 176/755

The Admiralty acquired a number of obsolete US Vought-Sikorsky Chesapeake dive-bombers in the hope of operating them from the new breed of escort carriers. However, their excessively long take-off run rendered them totally unsuitable and they were relegated to training. Seen here in 1941, AL918 is 'F' of 811 Squadron from Lee-on-Solent, which was intended but not destined to make the type operational.

FAAM ref: CHESAPEAKE/8

This airfield is RNAS Worthy Down, seen from 500 ft during camouflage tests with a mobile AA trailer code-named 'Scorpion' (arrowed) in July/August 1941. Much more interesting are the Fulmar, Lysander, Shark and Swordfish aircraft, some parked half-folded.

PRO ref: ADM 277/5

Fairey Albacore torpedo-cum-dive-bombers of 818 Squadron, not yet fitted with ASV radar, landing aboard *Formidable* in April 1942. The nearest aircraft is X9157 '5M' and is fitted with light-series carriers for flares or practice bombs.

PRO ref: ADM 186/801

*Albatross*, now HMS and not HMAS, sported this striking camouflage scheme, which included false bow and stern waves, while based at Freetown, Sierra Leone, after her 1941 refit at Simonstown, South Africa. Modifications included the addition of two quadruple pom-poms just abaft the funnel.

PRO ref: ADM 176/799

Once Japan had joined the Axis powers in the Second World War there was a risk that Vichy-France might allow the Japanese annexation of Madagascar, just as they had with Indo-China. To forestall this risk to the Cape route and the Indian Ocean, it was decided to mount Operation Ironclad; the occupation of the superb natural harbour at Diego Suarez. Vichy-French land, sea and air forces resisted and Swordfish of 829 Squadron from *Illustrious* torpedoed and sank the armed merchant cruiser *Bougainville* of 4,504 grt on 5 May 1942.

PRO ref: ADM 199/937

British losses were light, especially in air-to-air combat. Vichy-French losses included three Morane Saulnier 406C single-seat fighters, shot down by Martlets of 881 Squadron on 7 May. This example is No. 842 of Escadrille de Chasse 565, which made a particularly good crash-landing.

PRO ref: ADM 199/937

The Vichy-French sloop *D'Entrecasteaux*, 1,969 tons, was dive-bombed by Swordfish and strafed by fighters on several occasions on 5 and 6 May. Her crew managed to beach her to prevent her from sinking, thus enabling the wreck to be photographed on 9 May.

PRO ref: ADM 199/937

Following so soon after the fleet's heavy casualties in the Mediterranean during 1941, Japan's entry into the war caused available resources to be spread pitifully thin. Within six months, Japanese forces had inflicted further unaffordable losses, including two capital ships, a carrier and three heavy cruisers, together with Australian, Dutch and US units. A scratch Eastern Fleet was thrown together, with a nucleus of one or two new armoured carriers and supported by a hotch-potch of mainly second and third-class units. Among the faster vessels seen in Colombo Harbour in June/July 1942 are the battleship HMS *Warspite*, the light cruiser *Gambia* and an armoured carrier, either *Formidable* or *Illustrious*.

PRO ref: ADM 199/1389

Operation Pedestal was the great convoy of early August 1942 which finally lifted the siege of Malta. A large part of the convoy was caught by the camera on 9 August, just to the west of Gibraltar. As well as units of the convoy itself, much of the escort is also present, including at least three cruisers, the 16-in battleships *Nelson* and *Rodney*, and the carriers *Eagle* (foreground), *Furious* and *Argus*. It was at about this time that *Furious* transferred her Sea Hurricanes to *Argus*, which then returned to the UK, to make space for RAF Spitfires bound for Malta, which would be embarked at Gibraltar. Smoke from the funnel-less *Argus* and *Furious* is seen discharging from their aft vents.

PRO ref: ADM 199/1242

The August Malta convoy proved very costly, with most of the merchant ships and many of the escorting warships being sunk or damaged. On the afternoon of 11 August, U-73 put four torpedoes into the *Eagle*. No vessel of that age could have been expected to withstand such heavy underwater damage and the gallant old ship sank in less than eight minutes. In these four views she is turning over to port.

PRO ref: ADM 199/1242

The loss of *Eagle*, together with combat attrition, seriously weakened the Pedestal convoy's defences, and on the 12 August a raid by over one hundred German and Italian aircraft was aimed at the carriers *Indomitable* and *Victorious* (*Furious* having flown off her Spitfires and departed). The former, heavily damaged by two direct hits and two near-misses, is on fire, fore and aft. An escorting AA cruiser is astern and a Sea Hurricane is overhead.

PRO ref: ADM 199/1242

With her fires quenched, *Indomitable*'s damage is clearly seen. There is damage aft of the rear lift, while the forward lift is bowed and displaced above flight deck level. A large section of her starboard side adjacent to the forward lift has been blown out. Amazingly, emergency repairs enabled flying to continue. In this vessel an extra half-hangar enabled aircraft complement to be increased by a third, compared to the three 'Illustrious' class ships.

PRO ref: ADM 199/1242

Without the huge contribution made by women to the war effort in many spheres, neither of the world wars could have been won. Leading Wren Pat Lees got closer to the action than most, as this twenty-one-year-old radio mechanic was the first member of the WRNS to fly as part of her regular duties. She was photographed on 25 September 1942 beside Westland Lysander V9574 'W6U', a TT.IIIA of 755 Squadron at Worthy Down.

FAAM ref: 6 WR/5 × 4/6

A large number of escort carriers, based on slow mercantile hulls, were supplied by the United States. They could accommodate some twenty aircraft. HMS *Biter*, ex-*Rio Parana* of 8,200 tons, was the third of these, having commissioned on 4 May 1942. She is seen here, still in American waters at the Navy Yard New York, on 28 May. The four diesel-powered ships of this first group featured serious design flaws, about 1,000 tons of ballast being needed for stability. Problems with ammunition and aviation fuel storage led to the cataclysmic loss of two of them; *Avenger* and *Dasher*. *Biter* was later transferred to France and became the *Dixmude*.

PRO ref: ADM 176/863

An Albacore of 820 Squadron on *Formidable* during Operation Torch in November 1942. Because of anti-British feelings over Mers-el-Kebir (one would never think that it was the Germans who had invaded France in three consecutive wars), FAA aircraft were marked with US white-blue-yellow stars; serial numbers were painted out on British types and 'Royal Navy' replaced by 'US Navy'. Aircraft 'ØL' (BF653) is being loaded with six 250 lb semi-armour-piercing bombs.

FAAM ref: ALBACORE/10

The Fairey Seafox was a light catapult reconnaissance floatplane, deployed aboard some armed merchant cruisers and some smaller. Only sixty-six were built and it remains a little-known aircraft, but one example won fame spotting for Commodore Harwood's cruisers at the Battle of the River Plate in December 1939. This example is L4530, based in Bermuda and at one time attached to 773 Squadron, a Fleet Requirements Unit. The date is approximately mid-war, and the aircraft has what appears to be some sort of badge or emblem painted between the C1-type fuselage roundel and the serial number.

FAAM ref: FAIREY SEAFOX/17

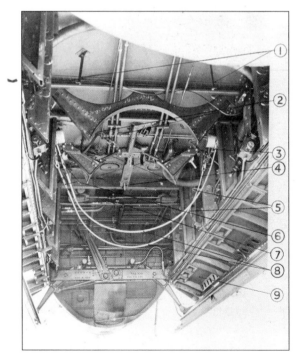

The US Grumman Avenger torpedo-bomber was originally known as the Tarpon in the Fleet Air Arm. This example was used at TDU Gosport in June 1943 for trials to test loading arrangements for the US Mk.13 Mod 1, 22.4-in torpedo. However, the FAA made no use of the Avenger as a torpedo bomber. This view shows the torpedo crutches and bomb bay details.

1. Forward Crutch Supports
2. Elastic Sling Retractor
3. Shackle
4. Stop Bolt
5. Engagement Loops
6. Turn-buckles
7. Forward Lug
8. Torpedo Slings
9. Recesses (P & S) for Box Air Tail

NB. Certain transverse components were reversed to accomodate various weapons fits.

PRO ref: AVIA 16/86

The *Empire Macalpine* of 7,950 grt was the first of many Merchant Aircraft Carriers, designed to provide anti-submarine cover for convoys, using Swordfish aircraft, A modified grain ship (some other MAC ships were modified tankers), she sailed with her first convoy on 29 May 1943.

PRO ref: ADM 199/1492

While operating off Sicily in support of Operation Husky on the night of 16 July 1943, HMS *Indomitable* (23,080 tons) was torpedoed on the port side amidships by a lone Ju 88; every torpedo pilot's dream of a perfect hit. In this view of the damage, looking aft, displaced 4½ in armour plates are evident. The hole in her side measured 28 ft by 25 ft. It appears that the German aircraft was mistaken for a returning Albacore and it escaped in the dark without a shot being fired at it. Counter-flooding was officially frowned on, but it helped right the ship's list (and might have saved *Ark Royal* in 1941) and enabled her to make 14 knots for Malta within 45 minutes of the attack. Aircraft were being operated again next day.

PRO ref: ADM 267/27

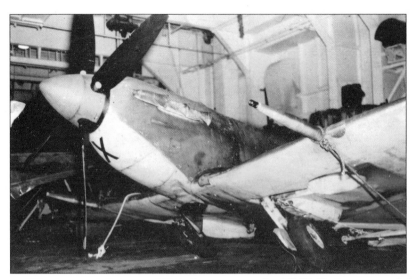

During passage to Gibraltar on 4–5 August 1943, the escort carrier HMS *Hunter* was struck by a gale which expensively revealed that her aircraft were not adequately secured in her hangar. Hardly any of the seventeen aircraft, six Seafires and six Swordfish of 834 Squadron, plus three Martlets and two Seafires on passage to Gibraltar, escaped damage. The undercarriage of Seafire LIIC NM939 'X' has collapsed and caused it to hit another (LR705 'Y'), which ended up in the lift well.

PRO ref: ADM 1/15068

In the same gale, Martlet Mk.IV FN111, being delivered to Gibraltar, broke loose after being hit by Seafire NM966 'Z' and damaged Swordfish Mk.II LS181 '4B'; in turn this hit another (HS299 'J'). The wrecked Swordfish in the foreground is Mk.II HS618 'C'.

PRO ref: ADM 1/15068

This is neither the same ship nor the same occasion. However, it does illustrate what a severe gale could do to an escort carrier. The ship is HMS *Stalker* and she is being tossed in a south-west gale while escorting convoy ON 223 during mid-February 1944.

PRO ref: ADM 199/70

All air forces lost depressingly large numbers of aircraft during training. Hawker Sea Hurricane Mk.IB AF952 of 804 Squadron was wrecked as a result of a flapless landing at RNAS Eglinton on

23 September 1943. The pilot, Sub-Lieutenant R.J. Wilson RNZNVR, was not badly injured.

PRO ref: ADM 207/8

The US Grumman Hellcat, originally known as the Gannet in the Fleet Air Arm, was one of the great fighters of the Second World War. 804 Squadron undertook deck landing training with its new mounts on board the escort carrier HMS *Ravager* in the autumn of 1943. Sub-Lieutenant W.E. 'Taffy' Adams brought Mk.I FN356 'E' in slightly too high, caught the last wire, and nearly got away with it. . .

PRO ref: ADM 207/8

. . . but not quite. The plane was repaired after this encounter with *Ravager*'s barrier. The date is 18 October 1943.

PRO ref: ADM 207/8

The development of weapons went on both despite and because of the war. The US had developed the first anti-submarine homing torpedo, the Mk.19 (cryptically referred to as the Mk.24 Mine), and made a number available to British forces. They were tested for use by Swordfish, which employed them with some success from escort carriers. Preliminary trials were conducted by the Aircraft Torpedo Development Unit (formerly the Torpedo Development Unit) at Gosport. Drop No. 8 took place on 9 December 1943.

PRO ref: ADM 1/12528
CN 1/5

The stubby torpedo, known widely as 'Fido', makes a good entry after drop No. 4 on 2 December. The box air tail, which detached on striking the sea, is clearly visible.

PRO ref: ADM 1/12528
CN 1/5

The first wave of strike aircraft crosses typical Norwegian terrain on 3 April 1944, as Operation Tungsten, the dive-bombing raid against the German battleship *Tirpitz* (42,900 tons, eight × 38-cm guns) in Kaafjord, gets underway. These are Barracudas of 8 Torpedo-Bomber-Reconnaissance Wing from HMS *Furious* and *Victorious*. Together with 52 TBR Wing, which followed an hour later, they secured fourteen hits which caused extensive damage and 438 casualties. The camera aircraft is carrying two × 500 lb SAP bombs, while the machine in the foreground has a single US-pattern 1,600 lb armour-piercing bomb.

PRO ref: ADM 199/1492

A number of 'Bogue' class escort carriers were transferred from the US Navy, becoming the 'Smiter' class in the Royal Navy. When not more actively employed, both RN and USN ships were often used for ferrying various types of aircraft; Avengers, Hellcats, Wildcats and P-40s in this case. The sister-ship in the background is loaded with P-39s, while on the quay are some Dauntlesses.

PRO ref: ADM 199/1492

On 17 May 1944 a mixed force of aircraft from **HMS** *Illustrious* and **USS** *Saratoga* attacked the docks and oil refineries at Surabaja, Java during Operation Transom. Spectacular fires and explosions were clear indications that the refinery and dockyard had received considerable damage, despite pessimistic reports. This was the first occasion on which FAA Avengers had attacked a land target.

PRO ref: ADM 199/341 f85

CN 1/40

The only legible part of this 850 Squadron Avenger's serial number is FN9, the last two digits having been overpainted by the rearmost white D-Day stripe. Another view reveals the code letter 'H' on its nose. This minor accident occurred on 15 August 1944 at Maydown, and therefore must have involved FN914, which skidded after its brakes jammed.

PRO ref: ADM 207/33

Fairey Barracuda Mk.II P9795 had '/G' marked after its serial number to denote that it was an experimental aircraft which should be under guard at all times when not in use. It was attached to the Airborne Forces Experimental Establishment, Beaulieu, during August and September 1944 for tests with under-wing 'Cuda' containers. The object on the torpedo crutches may be a fuel tank. What appear to be the original (and troublesome) long exhausts are in fact a special fit to reduce glare for night-flying.

PRO ref: AVIA 46/27

This view shows the rear doors of the port side container being opened. The 'Cuda' containers were designed to each carry two fully-armed paratroops, who would be dropped automatically by the pilot through the trap doors shown: pin-point accuracy was theoretically assured. Although successful live drops were made, the psychological effect on men cooped up in the containers was so great that the scheme was abandoned – presumably to the relief of all concerned.

PRO ref: AVIA 46/27

The German aircraft depot ship *Karl Meyer* of some 900 tons under rocket attack by Fairey Firefly Mk.I fighter-reconnaissance aircraft of 1771 Squadron from HMS *Implacable*. This was during Operation Athletic off Rörvik on 26 October 1944.

PRO ref: ADM 199/1492

On 27 November, *Implacable*'s Air Group (Barracudas of 828 Squadron and Fireflies of 1771 Squadron) mounted a successful attack on a German convoy in Alst Fjord. Several ships were hit, including the troop transport *Rigel* (1), of 3,828 grt. What appears to be at least one torpedo track is leading to the burning transport. Disturbance on the water indicates that the small vessel off *Rigel*'s starboard beam, possibly an armed trawler (flak ship) (2), is also under attack.

PRO ref: ADM 199/1492

'Merchant Navy' proclaims the tail marking on Swordfish Mk.II LS276. Piloted by Sub-Lieutenant H. Beckett, it served as 'E2' of 836 Squadron P Flight, which operated aboard the MAC ships MV *Adula* and later MV *Miralda* from September 1944 to March 1945. The men of the Merchant Aircraft Carriers, which were cargo-carrying freighters or tankers with flight decks, regarded the embarked aircraft as part of *their* navy.

FAAM ref: SWFH/595

This mishap to a Fulmar NF.II was thought to have involved DR746 'B0H' from 784 Squadron, attached to 813 Squadron on HMS *Campania* (1944) during Arctic convoy duties. The date is therefore probably 24 March 1944. The AI radar aerials above the wings, together with the ports for four × 0.5-in heavy machine-guns, are clearly visible. Fortunately the fireman clad in the asbestos suit has no work to do on this occasion.

FAAM ref: FLMR/80

HMS *Colossus* (13,190 tons), completed on 16 December 1944, was the first of the highly-successful light fleet carriers, which could accommodate up to forty aircraft and were built in numbers to mercantile standards, to enter service. However, she had not participated in any operations before the war ended. *Colossus* became the French *Arromanches* on 6 August 1946.

PRO ref: ADM 199/1492.

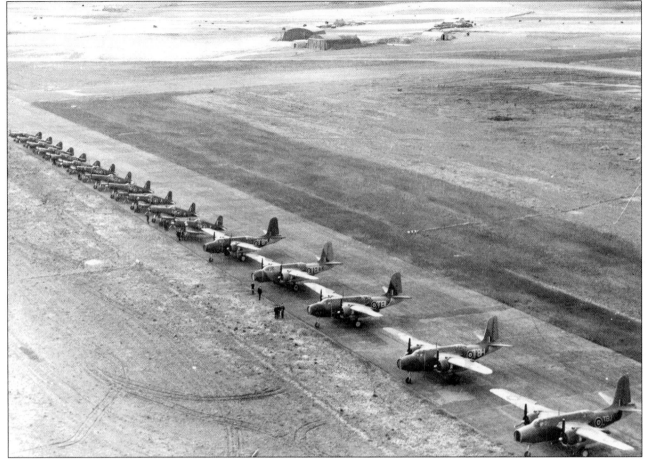

A long-serving unit at RNAS Twatt, the most northerly of the four Orkney airfields, was 771 Squadron, a Fleet Requirements Unit. Seen here in early 1945 is the squadron's full complement of Chance Vought Corsair Mk.II single-seat fighters, Miles Martinet TT. I target tugs and Douglas Boston Mk.III Turbinlite (former night fighter) aircraft, all wearing T8-series codes. Identifiable aircraft include Bostons W8255 'T8H', W8341 'T8L', W8369 'T8D' and W8396 'T8M'.

PRO ref: ADM 116/5790

The first helicopter in British service was the Sikorsky R-4 Hoverfly Mk.I. This example is FT836 from 771 Squadron and is seen landing at Rinnigill on the island of Hoy, the main radar station of the fleet base at Scapa Flow. The helicopter was used to take repair and maintenance staff to remote radar satellite sites during 1945. It is still wearing code letter 'A', which was allocated during familiarization training in the USA.

PRO ref: ADM 116/5790

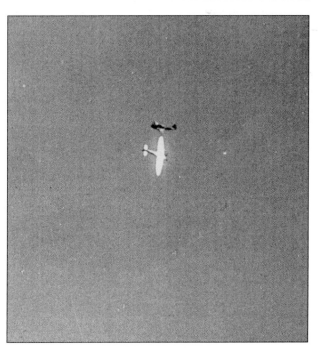

Kamikaze! A Mitsubishi A6M3, known to the Allies as a Zeke 32, outturns Sub-Lieutenant R.H. Reynolds' Supermarine Seafire of 887 Squadron, moments before crashing onto HMS *Indefatigable* (26,125 tons) on Easter Sunday, 1 April 1945. This was the first such hit on the British Pacific Fleet. The carrier was operating as part of Task Force 57 off Sakishima guntō during Operation Iceberg, the neutralization of the islands' airfields during the American assault on Okinawa.

PRO ref: ADM 199/595

The Zeke 32, carrying a 250 kg bomb, hit the base of *Indefatigable*'s island, causing many casualties and local damage. However, the armoured flight deck received nothing more than dishing over a small area, and flying operations were resumed in less than an hour. The dark patch on the smoke-blackened island is shadow below the new platform carrying two twin 20-mm AA guns. She and *Implacable* were the last of the armoured carriers derived from the 'Illustrious' concept and had hangar accommodation enlarged for fifty-four aircraft.

PRO ref: ADM 199/595

Experiments with floating airfields culminated in a series of live trials during 1945. The scheme was called Project Lily and the semi-flexible buoyant steel surface was constructed from hundreds of hexagonal sections, each six feet across the flats. On 27 April 1945, this Swordfish revealed that an aircraft caused local depressions in the runway.

PRO ref: ADM 1/20052

With a 9,000 lb fully-laden stationary aircraft, the depression in the 500 ft by 60 ft floating runway was much more severe than that shown on the previous plate. The effect would have been the equivalent of running uphill during both take-off and landing. This Swordfish Mk.III carries ASV Mk.XI below the fuselage, two × 250 lb depth charges, eight rocket rails and RATOG candles. The date is 25 September 1945.

PRO ref: ADM 1/20052

WRNS were trained to undertake all levels of aircraft servicing. This photograph, taken during May 1945, shows air mechanics working on a Martinet at RNAS Twatt.

FAAM ref: PERS/2200

The last Fleet Air Arm strike in northern waters, Operation Judgement, took place on 4 May 1945 at Kilbotn in the Lofotens. It was a field day for the escort carriers, the participating aircraft being sixteen Avengers and twenty-eight Wildcats from HMS *Queen, Searcher* and *Trumpeter*. The 5,035 grt U-boat depot ship *Black Watch* is exploding in the background, hidden by the headland, after being hit by several bombs. U-711, alongside her, was also sunk. In the middle-ground the 860 grt transport *Karl Von Hering* is being bombed and sunk. The warship in the left foreground is the Kriegsmarine AA ship *Thetis* of 3,858 tons; armed with seven × 10.5-cm, two × 4-cm and nine × 2-cm guns, she was formerly the British-built coast-defence ship HNoMS *Harald Haarfagre*. She was set on fire and her guns were largely silenced by the Wildcats.

PRO ref: ADM 199/1492

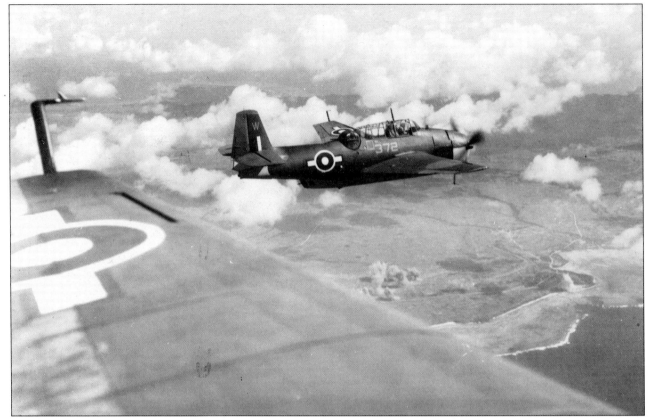

Avengers from *Indomitable* bomb Ishigaki shima airfield on 9 May 1945. Bombs can be seen bursting on the runway, below Mk.II JZ614 '372/W' of 857 Squadron.

PRO ref: ADM 199/590

The following three photos are from a series showing trial installations of various external stores on the Seafire Mk.III PR314 during the spring of 1945. Although the Seafire was satisfactory in the air, it was really too fragile to be a successful carrier aircraft. To burden it as shown was surely to provide straws for the camel's back. All stores were reported to affect stability adversely.

(*Above*) Two × 200 lb smoke floats underwing, plus a 45 imperial gallon fuel tank below the fuselage. This was the heaviest condition, take-off weight being 8,010 lbs: cleared for operational use.

PRO ref: AVIA 18/736

(*Right*) One 500 lb A Mk.VIII magnetic mine below fuselage: not cleared for operational use.

PRO ref: AVIA 18/736

(*Above*) Twelve 30 lb incendiary bombs, including four below the fuselage: cleared for operational use.

PRO ref: AVIA 18/736

(*Opposite, bottom*) This superb aerial view of RNAS North Front, Gibraltar, was taken on 28 June 1945. 779 Squadron's hangar and other accommodation is in the centre foreground. Several of the squadron's Beaufighter, Beaufort, Martinet and Seafire aircraft can be seen, together with 32 ft span winged targets. Excluding the RAF Warwicks on the runway, other types present include a Swordfish and possibly Sea Hurricanes.

FAAM ref: A/STN 385

Incredibly, in view of the size of the Imperial Japanese Navy, only one of its major warships was successfully attacked by Fleet Air Arm aircraft. On 24 July 1945, a group of ten Avengers, Corsairs and Fireflies found the 11,800 ton Merchant Aircraft Carrier *Shimane Maru*, converted from a standard 10,000 grt Type ITL War Standard tanker hull, eleven miles north-west of Oita. As usual, the Avengers went in too high and most bombs missed. However, her back was broken, possibly by near misses. Sub-Lieutenant F. Cawood of 849 Squadron from *Victorious* was on target and his bombs wrecked the ship forward, causing a serious fire. The dark shapes on deck may be casualties. Until recently it was thought that this vessel was the *Kaiyo*.

FAAM ref: CARS S/84

VJ Day on board HMS *Implacable*, 26,125 tons, with the ship dressed overall. Firefly FR. 1s of 1771 Squadron, including MB517 '274/N', are in the foreground, with a Walrus aft. Note the extra anti-Kamikaze Bofors guns on the island.

FAAM ref: CARS I/189

# ALARMS, EXCURSIONS AND TECHNOLOGICAL TRIUMPH

Corsair II JT622, still marked as '125/P' of 1834 Squadron from *Victorious*, where it was first damaged, is seen aboard the ferry carrier HMS *Pioneer*; it was damaged again, during 1946. It was not repaired. The artist is RM or Army.

FAAM ref: CRSR/103

The famous *Illustrious* is seen here in 1947, with additional radar, a revised light AA armament which included seventeen × 40-mm Bofors guns and an almost complete elimination of round-downs fore and aft of the useable flight deck. A Seafire and a Sea Fury are in evidence.

FAAM ref: CARS I/78

The Fairey Barracuda TR.V was the last and most capable of the series, but appeared too late for the war and most were cancelled. Powered by a Rolls-Royce Griffon 37 engine of 2,020 h.p., strengthened and with increased wing area, it was the only Mark to be cleared for flight deck operations with a 2,000 lb AP bomb, with which it would have been a formidable dive-bomber. Only thirty-two were built, mostly serving with second-line units. This example, with heightened fin, is RK568 '281/C' of HMS *Implacable*'s Ship's Flight in the early summer of 1948.

FAAM ref: BARA/117

Landing problems due to a failure to pick up arrester wires caused many costly and often tragic accidents. Safety barriers to halt runaway aircraft were effective but could themselves often cause damage and sometimes casualties. A review of safety barrier engagements by different types of Naval aircraft between October 1948 and October 1950 was conducted by RAE Farnborough. It was concluded that a three-wire barrier, set at the height appropriate to the type of aircraft, was reasonably effective with single-propeller tailwheel types, although double barriers offered better protection to the forward deck park. There remained a risk of damage to aircraft until 'long pull-out' units could be fitted. However, the incidence of fire and injury was assessed as very satisfactory. Some of the many types of landing incidents illustrated are shown here and overleaf.

(*Above*) Seafire F.17 SX165 '115/JA' of 1831 RNVR Squadron, based ashore at RNAS Stretton, has floated over the wires and into the first barrier on *Illustrious* with its undercarriage on 22 September 1949. Surprisingly, the wooden propeller has damaged the steel wire barrier.

PRO ref: AVIA 54/1992

Fairey Firefly FR.I DK417 '205/VL' of 767 Squadron shore-based at RNAS Yeovilton has come to grief after a tail-down floating entry into *Illustrious*'s short pull-out barrier on 1 March 1950. The pilot, Lieutenant Commander J.W. Wellham, was a Taranto veteran.

PRO ref: AVIA 54/1992

## AIRSCREW

Blackburn Firebrand TF.5 EK625 '110/C' of 813 Squadron sheds propeller blades as it neatly engages *Implacable*'s barrier along the whole of its wingspan.

PRO ref: AVIA 54/1992

Despite her appearance, the 14,700 ton *Unicorn* was not designed as an operational carrier, although she served briefly as such during 1943. Her intended rôle was aircraft maintenance and ferrying; which is precisely what she was doing off the Korean coast in the summer of 1950. She was in fact supporting HMS *Triumph*, whose Seafires and Fireflies were the first British aircraft in action during the Korean War. A DUKW coded DW72 is on deck, together with a Seafire FR.47 and several Firefly FR.1s, including PP481.

FAAM ref: CARS U/20

Given its position relative to the photographer, this 800 Squadron Seafire FR.47, with everything down, may be on an overshoot. Part of *Triumph*'s air group on Korean War duties between 1 June and 22 July 1950, VP493 '174/P' carries long-range fuel tanks.

FAAM ref: SFR/324

This Supermarine Sea Otter ASR.2, from the Ship's Flight of a sister-ship, is on the light fleet carrier HMS *Theseus* off the coast of Korea. It is probably September or October 1950, as the Fireflies and Sea Furies astern have not yet received their distinctive UN black and white stripes. What the Americans made of the Sea Otter, in a war which saw combat between transonic jet fighters, can only be imagined!

FAAM ref: S/OTT 20

The Australian light fleet carrier HMAS *Sydney* took a turn on Korean War duties between September 1951 and January 1952. Here her flight deck forward is full of aircraft awaiting catapult launches, while Sea Fury FB.11 VX730 '109/K' of 805 Squadron is manhandled into position. The Sikorsky HO3S-1 coded 'UP-28' was loaned to *Sydney* by the US Navy.

FAAM ref: CARS S/50

The Korean winter of 1950–1 was particularly bitter. This is the snow-bound flight deck of *Theseus*, with a UN-striped Firefly FR.5 of 810 Squadron in the foreground to port and Sea Fury '126/T' of 807 Squadron to starboard.

FAAM ref: SEA FURY/159

The FAA operated no turbine-engined aircraft and therefore no fleet carriers during the Korean War. However, the Fireflies and Sea Furies (arguably more capable than the earliest jets) won great acclaim, as did the light fleet carriers. Here, a Firefly FR.5 of 810 Squadron on board HMS *Theseus* is shortly to deliver two 500 lb medium capacity bombs and a pair of 3-in rockets with 60 lb high-explosive warheads.

FAAM ref: ARMS/BMS 55

The advent of the Westland Wyvern, a heavy tail-dragger with contra-rotating propellers, placed new strains on arrester gear and barriers. A series of trials was conducted on board the new fleet carrier HMS *Eagle* (1951) of 36,800 tons, off Plymouth during 1952. Two TF.1s and two TF.2s were used. In all tests the barrier was engaged without suffering serious damage from the Wyverns' propellers. However, the aircraft themselves were all either wrecked or badly damaged. Collisions between the bent blades of the two propellers produced flying fragments which were dangerous to personnel. On 15 May, VP120, the only Rolls-Royce Clyde-equipped Wyvern TF.2 was used. After its propellers struck the steel deck, causing spectacular sparks, the fuselage failed behind the engine and the aircraft landed on its back. The remains ended up at Pendine Sands ranges after an incident with a low bridge en route.

PRO ref: AVIA 54/1992

Wyvnet or Ganvern? This is in fact Wyvern TF.1 VR133. New trials to find barriers suitable for carrier aircraft with contra-rotating propellers were conducted at RAE Farnborough. However, because no Gannet was available, VR133 was crudely modified to simulate both types by fitting a plywood profile of a Gannet cockpit and a nose strut with two Spitfire tail wheels. Even though it arrested the aircraft without damaging the propellers, the barrier was deemed a failure, as it was likely to injure aircrew by crushing cockpit canopies.

PRO ref: AVIA 54/1992

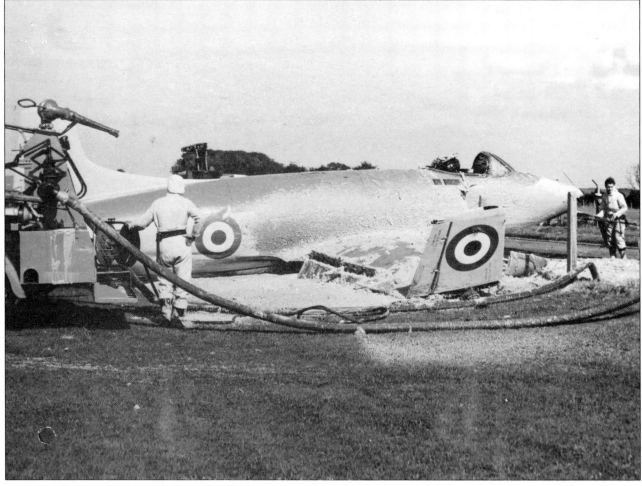

Among the most vital personnel on any carrier or airfield during flying operations are the fire-fighting crews. Supermarine Attacker FB.1 WA511 of 702 Squadron suffered fuel transfer valve problems, not uncommon in Attackers, and force-landed at RNAS Culdrose on 19 August 1952. Although a write-off, prompt action with foam spray prevented total destruction. The 590 m.p.h. Attacker, which first entered service in 1951, was the Fleet Air Arm's first operational jet.

PRO ref: ADM 1/25325

British scientists and engineers produced the angled flight deck, the steam catapult and the mirror landing aid for carriers. However, the Royal Navy was often slow in introducing radical new developments into service. This is the mirror landing aid, with its red and green lights; so important for safe landings in fast jets with high approach speeds and relatively unresponsive engines. It is seen installed in the trials carrier *Illustrious* on 25 November 1953.

PRO ref: ADM 1/25316

A tragic and fatal accident occurred on 22 February 1954. The pilot of Attacker FB.2 WP295 from 803 Squadron lost control after being catapulted from HMS *Eagle* off Gibraltar and the fighter hit the sea.

PRO ref: ADM 1/25322

The light fleet carrier HMS *Warrior*, 13,190 tons, is seen on a visit to Hong Kong in about April 1954. She has been modernised with an enclosed bridge, lattice mast, new radar and 40-mm Bofors armament. Ranged forward on deck are Hawker Sea Fury FB.11s of 811 Squadron,

including WE735 '115/J', WZ631 '101/J', WG596 '103/J', WJ223 '110/J', WM491 '105/J', WF594 '113/J' and VX621 '107/J'. Aft are Firefly AS.5s of 825 Squadron.

PRO ref: ADM 1/25564

Like all new aircraft types, the de Havilland Sea Venom FAW.20, the fleet's first jet all-weather fighter, underwent clearance checks for various weapons outfits. WH507 was cleared at A&AEE Boscombe Down between October 1954 and April 1955 for the carriage of eight 3-in rockets with 60 lb warheads. Performance limits were set at 45° dive angle and a speed of 575 m.p.h.

PRO ref: AVIA 18/1479

On 3 December 1954, Firefly AS.6 WB378 of 737 Squadron spun in on approach and crashed in shallow water on the edge of Lough Foyle, just off the end of the runway at RNAS Eglinton. The pilot suffered fatal injuries because suitable safety helmets were not available. Sub-Lieutenant I.Mc.A. Hardie quickly brought Westland Dragonfly Mk.3 WG723 to the scene and mounted a rescue operation. The Dragonfly, based on the US Sikorsky S-51, was the first British-built helicopter to serve with the Royal Navy.

PRO ref: ADM 1/25360

Although designed as a reconnaissance-bomber for planned new fleet carriers, changed requirements saw the Short Sturgeon relegated to the rôle of high-speed target tug. Most were used by 728 Squadron at RNAS Hal Far, Malta, which used the carrier-capable TT.2 between 1951 and 1956. This example, towing a 32 ft span winged target over the Mediterranean, is TS486 '591'.

FAAM ref: SHORT/142

This view of *Eagle*'s flight deck dates from late 1955 and illustrates the Fleet Air Arm's flirtation with turboprop bombers. The Wyvern S.4s are from two squadrons, 813 (striped maroon finlets) and 827 (red and green wyvern emblems), and include WL879 '127/J' (813), VZ789 '133/J' and WL883 '139/J' (827). They are about to set off to attack the target being towed behind the carrier. Each is carrying six 3-in rockets with 60 lb concrete warheads and two 500 lb MC bombs. In a shooting war the load could be doubled. The Fairey Gannet AS.1s parked aft on the port quarter are from 826 Squadron, and include WN428 '343/J', behind which is part of the mirror landing aid. Aircraft handling equipment is parked under the carrier's island.

FAAM ref: WYVN/69

A 2,000-lb AP bomb is loaded onto Wyvern S.4 WL888 '374/J' of 830 Squadron, on board HMS *Eagle* in 1956. The black colour suggests an inert example for training, in the same way blue is used today. First used by RAF Beauforts in May 1940, this excellent bomb was rendered obsolete only because delivery from medium altitude became suicidal.

FARM ref: BM/51

Senior officers on board the aircraft carrier HMS *Eagle* during the Suez intervention, which was code-named Operation Musketeer. Second left is Air Marshal Denis H.F. Barnett, Allied Air Task Force Commander; fifth left, Captain H.D.C. MacLean, in command of HMS *Eagle*; sixth left, Lieutenant-General Sir Hugh C. Stockwell, Land Task Force Commander.

PRO ref: DEFE 2/1794

Servicing between sorties on *Eagle*'s flight deck during the Suez emergency in late 1956. The Hawker Sea Hawks belong to 897 (foreground) and 899 Squadrons; the nearest aircraft being FGA. 6 XE381 '192/J'. Sea Venom FAW.21s of 892 Squadron are to port, with Douglas Skyraider AEW.1s of A Flight 849 Squadron aft, including WT984 '414A/J'.

FAAM ref: S/HWK 169

The Sea Hawk was an elegant little aircraft. This example is WM985 '463/B' of 895 Squadron, an ex-897 Squadron FB.3. Below can be seen HMS *Bulwark* (22,000 tons) with escorts.

FAAM ref: S/HWK 183

Sea Venom FAW.21 XG677 '221/Z' of 809 Squadron being marshalled forward for take-off on board HMS *Albion* in November 1956, during Operation Musketeer. This is a particularly colourful machine, with not only 'Suez' black and yellow stripes on the standard Extra Dark Sea Grey and Sky camouflage, but also both the squadron's phoenix badge on its nose and the fin panel in red, plus black and white tip tanks.

FAAM ref: CARS A/408

In this interesting example of cross-decking, Wyvern S.4 VZ795 '387/0' from 831 Squadron on *Ark Royal* (1955) is taxiing on board USS *Saratoga* (1956) alongside in harbour in June 1957. During an exercise the two carriers exchanged aircraft and in a minor accident, the Wyvern was slightly damaged and was retained on the American ship for repairs. It wears the squadron badge on its fin and a 'Flook' emblem below the cockpit.

FAAM ref: WYVN/43

This de Havilland Sea Vixen FAW.1 XJ586 '212/V' of 892 Squadron on HMS *Victorious* is well-protected against the tropical sun off Kuwait in July 1961, especially its plastic radome. The Sea Vixen was the first British fighter to dispense with guns and rely on guided missiles (four Firestreaks) for its primary air-to-air armament. The retractable launchers for 2-in unguided rockets and the blanked-off flight refuelling probe are noteworthy.

FAAM ref: S/VXN 168

A lucky escape! Meteor U.16 WF741 unmanned radio-controlled drone was used as a target for air-to-air firing on 26 October 1961. Amazingly, it survived a strike by a Firestreak guided missile, fired by a de Havilland Sea Vixen FAW.1 of 893 Squadron from HMS *Centaur*, and was guided safely back to RAE Llanbedr.

PRO ref: AVIA 13/1274

The Supermarine Scimitar became the fleet's first swept wing transonic aircraft when it joined the front line in 1958. This F.1, '156/V' of 803 Squadron on HMS *Victorious*, was used for trials with the AGM 12B Bullpup, a 10 ft 6 in long 571 lb air-to-ground guided missile, during February 1962. The first two missiles have been released but have not yet ignited. The object under the Scimitar's fuselage is probably a trials camera.

FAAM ref: BM/29

The hovercraft, the air-cushion vehicle invented by Christopher Cockerell in 1955, was seen as a totally new form of versatile transport, and possibly weapons platform, with wide but unknown potential. An Inter-Service Hovercraft Trials Unit was established at RNAS Lee-on-Solent in February 1962, although the crews were not Fleet Air Arm. Its task was to probe the capabilities of this revolutionary machine, using the SR-N1 during a fifteen-week trials period in the first half of that year. The machine's manoeuvrability, amphibious qualities and high speed of up to 55 knots were all demonstrated.

PRO ref: ADM 1/28993

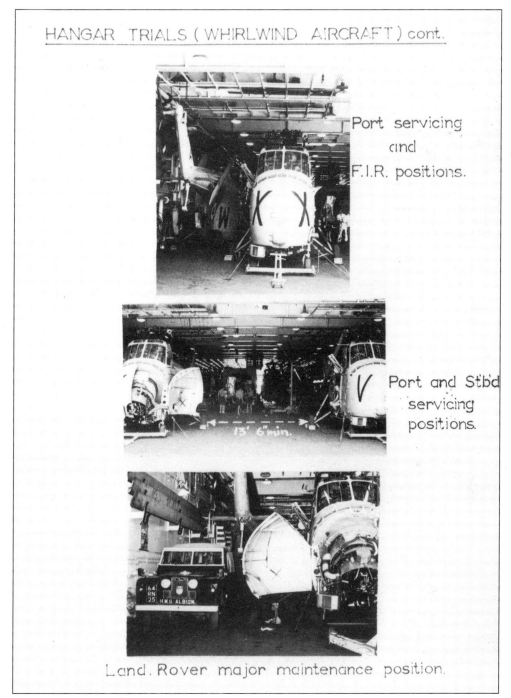

HANGAR TRIALS (WHIRLWIND AIRCRAFT) cont.

Port servicing and F.I.R. positions.

Port and St'b'd servicing positions.

Land. Rover major maintenance position.

Space for both vehicles and aircraft in the hangars of commando carriers was limited and therefore needed to be carefully managed. This series of photographs shows carefully-monitored trials underway in HMS *Albion* at the turn of 1962/3. The Westland Whirlwind HAS.7s, painted Light Stone with black lettering, belongs to 846 Squadron.

PRO ref: ADM 1/28732

Modifications had already altered the 1955 *Ark Royal* (43,340 tons) considerably, when photographed in the Mediterranean during May 1963. In particular, gone is the deck-edge lift and almost all of the guns forward of midships. Wessex helicopters, Scimitars and Sea Vixens are on deck.

PRO ref: DEFE 7/1717

XK534 '230/LM' of 809 Squadron, based at RNAS Lossiemouth during 1963, was one of the new Blackburn Buccaneer S.1 low-level strike aircraft. It could deliver an 8,000 lb bomb load at some 650 m.p.h. from sea level. As befitted its nuclear capability when carrying the 2,000 lb Red Beard tactical weapon, it was painted in anti-flash white.

PRO ref: DEFE 7/1717

The increasing reliance on helicopters led to the introduction of a new type of vessel; the helicopter support ship. The first was **HMS** *Lofoten* (2,140 tons), converted from tank landing ship LST 3027. She could accommodate up to six helicopters. All three Wessex HAS.1s of 737 Squadron, seen on deck in November 1963, have their rotors turning.

PRO ref: ADM 1/28613

On the night of 22/3 December 1963, the Greek cruise liner *Lakonia*, 20,314 grt, full of Christmas holidaymakers, caught fire 180 miles north of Madeira. Among the vessels which hastened to her aid was the carrier HMS *Centaur*. One of her helicopters, Whirlwind HAS.7 '977/C' of the Ship's Flight, moves between ships. Despite all these efforts, ninety-five passengers and thirty-three crew from the *Lakonia* perished.

PRO ref: ADM 1/28628

Although the Gannet AEW.3 normally had no offensive rôle, it was cleared to carry anti-submarine homing torpedoes. This is a 12.75-in US-designed Mk.44 light-weight (433 lb) torpedo on the starboard pylon of XL452 from 849 Squadron, some time in mid-1964. The parachute tail is steadied by an extension arm on the stores carrier. The dropping envelope was between 150 and 207 m.p.h. and from at least 500 ft.

PRO ref: AVIA 16/287

The remarkable pattern on the sea is caused by downwash from Wessex HAS.1 XPI38 'M/B' of 845 Squadron from HMS *Bulwark* (23,300 tons). The wet-suited crewman is about to plunge into the sea off Borneo as part of Air-Sea Rescue training in September 1964 during the Indonesian crisis.

FAAM ref: CARS B/92

HMS *Eagle* after her 1959–64 modernization, resulting in her tonnage shooting up to 44,100. Overshadowing her fully-angled flight deck and modern and highly capable aircraft complement of Wessex helicopters, Buccaneers, Gannets and Sea Vixens is the massive Type 984 radar. All Bofors guns have been replaced with Seacat guided missiles.

FAAM ref: CARS E/95

Many hands make safe work. Loading a Bullpup AGM 12B onto a Sea Vixen FAW.2 of 899 Squadron on board *Eagle* during 1965. The missile's control surfaces have yet to be fitted.

FAAM ref: BMS/61

848 Squadron Wessex HU.5 XS494 'P' sits unserviceable, with rotor servo problems, in a Borneo jungle clearing during 1965. Whirlwind 'T' is from the same unit.

FAAM ref: WSX/150

Conditions in the Borneo jungle could be so bad that special landing pads for helicopters had to be constructed from logs. This machine is Wessex HU.5 XS479 'A/A' of 848 Squadron from HMS *Albion*. It operated with Royal Marine Commandos during 1966.

FAAM ref: WESSEX/455

The commando carriers *Albion* (foreground) and *Bulwark* are seen here together off the coast of Borneo at the turn of 1965/6. Both are carrying Wessex helicopters, and *Albion*'s landing craft are also visible, suspended aft below flight deck level.

FAAM ref: CARS A/125

A UN Security Council resolution led to carrier operations which were designed to prevent crude oil for Rhodesia entering the port of Beira after the Rhodesian government's illegal unilateral declaration of independence. *Eagle* was on station during March and April 1966, and one of her 800 Squadron Buccaneer S.1s is inspecting the tanker *Joanna V*.

FAAM ref: BUCC/338

HMS *Eagle* at speed in 1966. Buccaneer S.1 XN962 '110/E', which has just landed and picked up a wire, is from 800 Squadron and Sea Vixen FAW.2 XP959 '132/E' is from 899 Squadron. Wessex helicopters hover in the distance.

FAAM ref: BUCC/337

In its tactical nuclear strike rôle during the 1960s, the Buccaneer carried the bulky 2,000 lb Red Beard weapon in a recess on the bomb bay door.

FAAM ref: ARMS/BMS 52

This historic machine is XT595, the first McDonnell Douglas Phantom for the RN. It is seen here during its first flight on 27 June 1966 over St Louis. This British version, the Phantom F-4K, and known as the FG.1 in the Fleet Air Arm, was powered by Rolls-Royce Spey 201 engines and had folding radomes and a number of other modifications which separated it from the US Navy's F-4B. Cut-backs in naval aviation led to the original order for 140 aircraft being reduced to a mere thirty eight. The Phantom was the Royal Navy's only supersonic aircraft.

FAAM ref: PHAN/96

The Westland Wasp HAS.1 was one of the great post-war successes among British-designed naval aircraft. As with Swordfish on auxiliary carriers during the Second World War, it enabled a deadly anti-submarine aircraft to be based on a wide range of smaller vessels. Armed with two homing torpedoes, it was designed to kill submarines detected by the parent ship. XT434 '444' is from the 829 Squadron detachment on the 'Tribal' class frigate HMS *Gurkha*, although the ship in the photograph is the 'Leander' class frigate HMS *Aurora*. The date is approximately 1965–7.

FAAM ref: WASP/29

On 18 March 1967 the 118,000 grt oil tanker *Torrey Canyon* ran onto the Seven Stones Reef. Much of her oil came ashore on the Cornish coast, but the remainder left in the wreck was burnt off by attacks by aircraft; Buccaneers of 736 and 800 Squadrons from RNAS Brawdy with 1,000 lb bombs, RAF Hunters with napalm and Sea Vixens from Yeovilton releasing aviation spirit at the end of Operation Mop-up. This is the wreck after the fires had burnt themselves out.

FAAM ref: CARS T/42

Even if not quite Fleet Air Arm, this is most definitely a Navy/aviation subject. Wishing to know how the Mk.44 torpedo would perform after launching from the Australian Ikara Mk.M4 rocket, which was shortly to be introduced into the Royal Navy, it was decided to launch one from an Ikara carried by a Canberra light bomber. The loaded Ikara was carried under the port wing of Canberra B(I).8 WT333 in August 1969, with cameras under the starboard wing. The loaded Ikara could be carried at up to 465 m.p.h.

PRO ref: AVIA 16/260

Crown Copyright. Reproduced with the permission of the Controller of HMSO.

Although Magnetic Anomaly Detection had been used by US forces during the Second World War to locate submerged submarines, British interest lagged behind. When interest developed, a portable system was sought for RN helicopters. Here, a MAD 'bird' is attached to a special carrier on a Westland Wasp HAS.1 in December 1969. This was carried in lieu of the starboard Mk.44 torpedo. The 70 in long 'bird' was streamed on a 150 ft cable, and the torpedo could be released without causing interference. The Wasp was a truly lightweight machine, weighing only 2,400 lbs empty.

PRO ref: AVIA 16/313

Crown Copyright. Reproduced with the permission of the Controller of HMSO.

# INTO THE MILLENIUM

Royal Navy Sea Kings rescued forty crewmen from the US cargo ship *Steel Vendor*, 8,114 grt, which ran aground in the South China Sea on 7 October 1971. This HAS.1 is '140/E' of 826 Squadron from *Eagle*.

FAAM ref: S/KING 479

Following the Turkish occupation of Northern Cyprus in the summer of 1974, Sea Kings of 814 Squadron evacuated a number of British tourists and took them to HMS *Hermes* (1959). This Sea King is HAS.1 XV700 '272/H'.

FAAM ref: S/KING 505

Well before the 1970s it was usual for major warships to have helicopters embarked. Large ships, such as the 5,440 ton guided-missile destroyer HMS *Hampshire*, carried the Wessex. HAS.3 XS153 is '402/HA' of the Ship's Flight, part of 737 Squadron. Named 'Humphrey', it wears a hippo emblem on the lower nose and is taking part in a Search and Rescue competition on 15 January 1975.

FAAM ref: WSX/454

Portland sea training was a by-word among the world's navies. Hovering over HMS *Juno*, HNMS *Friesland*, the Nigerian *Otobo* and a 'Sabre' class fast training boat is Wasp XV626 '472' of the Ship's Flight HMS *Andromeda* element of 829 Squadron during May 1976.

FAAM ref: WASP/263

Ready for inspection! Modernized again to become the Royal Navy's only carrier capable of operating the McDonnell Douglas Phantom, *Ark Royal*, her tonnage now 43,060, is seen here with Phantom FG.1s of 892 Squadron, Buccaneer S.2s of 809 Squadron, a Gannet AEW.3 of 849 Squadron B-Flight, a couple of Sea Kings and a Wessex.

FAAM ref: CARS A/437

An unusual and slightly later view of *Ark Royal*, with Sea Kings of 824 Squadron strongly in evidence, but no Wessex. The three Gannets can be identified as XL497 '041/R', XL450 '042/R' and XL471 '043/R'. Note the ship's boats adding to the clutter along the starboard edge of the flight deck.

FAAM ref: CARS A/438

*Ark Royal*'s upper and lower hangars on 3 and 5 decks, containing Buccaneer and Phantom aircraft. Buccaneer S.2s include XV869 '020/R' and XV332 '026/R' in the background, while '024/R' in the lower right foreground is XN982.

FAAM ref: CARS A/439

In an attempt to get more heavy helicopters to sea, two of the three obsolete 'Tiger' class light cruisers were converted into ugly cruiser/carriers, with a flight deck and hangar for four aircraft aft. This is HMS *Blake*: *Lion* was scrapped early and unconverted. *Blake*'s dual capability (she was the last RN unit with 6-in guns) would have proved invaluable during the Falklands conflict, but she was not deployed. The cruiser's four 820 Squadron Union Flag-bedecked Sea King HAS.2s are XZ575 '(4)10/BL', XV696 '(4)11/BL', XV647 '(4)12/BL' and XV671 '(4)13/BL, seen over the ship in April 1977.

FAAM ref: SK/330

Heavy maintenance. An engine change for a British Aerospace Sea Harrier is a major task which entails total removal of the aircraft's wing structure. This FRS.1 is XZ458 '251/N' of 800 Squadron, seen in HMS *Invincible*'s hangar during 1980. These relatively small ships normally carry only some fifteen aircraft.

FAAM ref: S/HARRIER 150

Whenever they approached the British coast or British forces, Russian snoopers were intercepted and politely but firmly escorted away. None were more impressive than the mighty Tupolev 95 'Bear', the unique turboprop inter-continental bomber with its 12,000+ km range. Sea Harrier FRS.1 XZ498 '005/N' from *Invincible*'s 801 Squadron, shadowing this 'D' variant in 1981, has dummy Sidewinder missiles, but its podded 30-mm cannon might be loaded.

FAAM ref: S/HARRIER 151

Flight deck conditions on smaller warships can be very difficult. This anti-submarine torpedo-armed Westland Lynx HAS.2 is from the Ship's Flight of the destroyer HMS *Birmingham* (3,500 tons); part of 702 Squadron. It is engaged on trials of the Harpoon helicopter tie-down system, the grid for which is visible below the aircraft.

FAAM ref: LYNX/130

Operation Corporate is still generally better known as the Falklands conflict. At dawn on 29 April 1982 the Argentinian submarine *Santa Fe*, 1,870 tons, was caught on the surface by helicopters from a number of RN vessels. She ran aground in a damaged condition at Bas Jetty, Grytviken. An 829 Squadron Wasp from HMS *Endurance*, one of the units which attacked her, is seen overhead.

FAAM ref: FALKLANDS/284

A Sea Harrier of 800 Squadron leaves the ski ramp on *Hermes* while another, plus two Sea Kings, shelters to starboard. Only just subsonic, the Sea Harrier proved to be a deadly fighter and useful ground attack aircraft. The wide variety of vehicles and the ready-to-use weapons for the Sea Harriers and Sea Kings, including 1,000 lb MC bombs, Sidewinder AAMs, 250 lb depth charges, rocket and cannon pods and homing torpedoes, are noteworthy.

FAAM ref: FALKLANDS/275

In very murky conditions east of the Falklands, a Sea King HAS.2 of 825 Squadron approaches the *Queen Elizabeth II* on 27 May 1982, with the cloud base down to below funnel level. A laden Sea King is pulling away from the liner, which had two heli-platforms fitted, but retained her peace-time colour scheme.

FAAM ref: FALKLANDS/166

Sidewinder-armed Sea Harrier FRS.1 XZ460 '26', from 800 Squadron on HMS *Hermes*, and Harrier GR.3 XZ992 '05', of the RAF's 1 Squadron, overfly the supply ship RFA *Stromness* and the tanker RFA *Bayleaf* in June 1982.

FAAM ref: FALKLANDS 10

A hero's, or should it be heroine's, return. HMS *Hermes* docks at Portsmouth on 21 July 1982 on her return from the Falklands conflict. Every size and shape of small craft escorted her in, and countless people lined the Portsmouth sea front from Southsea to the naval base. The throng here is waiting to greet loved ones; the brows are ready for positioning, a Royal Marines band is at the ready, and her crew are manning ship. The air group appears to comprise fifteen Sea Kings, two Lynx and six Sea Harriers. The *Hermes* was the last Royal Navy fighting ship of over 20,000 tons standard displacement. She now serves with the Indian Navy as the *Viraat*.

FAAM ref: FALKLANDS/285

One of the greatest disadvantages suffered by the fleet during the Falklands campaign was a lack of airborne early warning. Urgent steps to rectify this deficiency led to the Sea King AEW.2 with Searchwater radar. This machine is XV650 '180' of 849 Squadron, rebuilt from WA638. The Sea King has proved to be even more of a multi-rôle aircraft than its predecessor, the Wessex.

FAAM ref: S/KING 504

Among the aircraft of the Fleet Requirements and Air Direction Unit, operated by the civilian-manned AirWork, were colourful English Electric Canberra target tugs. This TT.18 is WJ614 '846'.

FAAM ref: EE/30

(*Opposite, bottom*) HMS *Invincible*, 16,256 tons, in the midst of a tumultuous welcome home as she passes the historic Round Tower guarding the entrance to Portsmouth Harbour. Her Majesty the Queen waits to greet her on her return home from war on 17 September 1982. Her air group appears to comprise seven Sea Harriers and eleven Sea Kings.

FAAM ref: CARS I/199

The last of the three 'Invincible' class light carriers, *Ark Royal* (1985), 16,256 tons, incorporated several post-Falklands improvements, including a steeper ski ramp and additional AA guns (such as the 20-mm Phalanx gatling gun on her port quarter). It was originally intended that she would be called *Indomitable*, which would not only have been alliterative with *Invincible* and *Illustrious*, but

would also have been a fitting tribute to the famous carrier which did so much during the Second World War. She is seen entering Fort Lauderdale in July 1986.

FAAM ref: CARS A/441

During Operation Granby, better known as the Gulf War, the White Ensign flies proudly at 848 Squadron's headquarters 'somewhere in the desert'. The unit's UN-striped Sea Kings 'WN' and 'WO' are prominent.

FAAM ref: GRANBY/3

Seen over desert fire trenches during their deployment for Operation Granby, these Sea King HC.4s of 845 Squadron clearly display their United Nations black and white stripes. The two nearest aircraft are coded 'P' and 'N'. Large air filters are fitted in front of the engine intakes.

FAAM ref: GRANBY/4

The threat from ground-to-air missile attack was ever-present. ZG821 'WE', one of the commando force's Sea King HC.4s of 848 Squadron, is demonstrating decoy flares over the Saudi desert.

FAAM ref: S/KING 503

Royal Navy helicopters conducted successful anti-shipping operations on 30 January 1991. One of the victims was this Russian-built 500 ton 'T 43' type mine-warfare vessel, possibly the *Al Kadisia*. She was hit at 1156 local time, by a Sea Skua missile fired from Westland Lynx XZ720 '410' of HMS *Gloucester*'s Ship's Flight, and was still burning twelve hours later.

FAAM ref: GRANBY/2

The Lynx helicopter/Sea Skua missile weapons system proved itself deadly. This is Lynx XZ720 '410' of HMS *Gloucester* Flight, 815 Squadron, which sank at least two enemy vessels during Operation Granby. There are in fact four claim tallies below the cockpit. Lieutenant Commander D. Livingstone was the pilot and Lieutenant M.F. Ford RN, his observer.

FAAM ref: LYNX/137

*Ark Royal*, in the foreground, and *Illustrious* (1982) training together off Portland on 26 January 1994. *Illustrious*, with radomes removed, carries three of the new Goalkeeper gatling-type 30 mm AA close-in weapons system.

FAAM ref: CARS A/442

(*Opposite, bottom*) Operation Haven was a multi-national humanitarian effort to assist an estimated half a million Kurdish refugees, victims of Saddam Hussein, on the Iraqi-Turkish border in the spring and early summer of 1991. The flight deck of RFA *Argus* (1988) of 18,280 tons, (note AA guns temporarily mounted at rear of island) carries equipment and black and white (UN) striped helicopters for the Royal Marines.

FAAM ref: CARS A/440

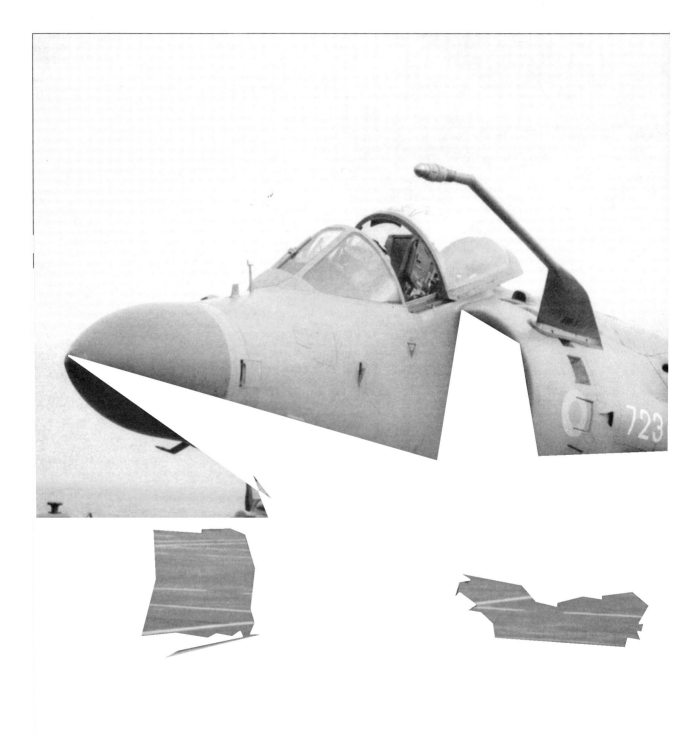

The FAA's latest fixed-wing aircraft is the Sea Harrier FA.2. 899 Squadron was the first to convert to this potent new version of the incredible Harrier family, acting as the Operational Evaluation Unit. Wearing the squadron's mailed fist emblem on its fin, the nearest aircraft is ZD615, coded '723/OEU'. The new and highly

capable Blue Vixen radar is immediately evident. With its potent new AMRAAM missiles, the FA.2 now equips 800 and 801 Squadrons, and has seen active service on peacekeeping duties over the former Yugoslavia.

FAAM ref: S/HARRIER 149

The big Sea King has been the invaluable workhorse of the FAA for many years. Nowhere has it proved more useful than in former Yugoslavia, serving mainly as a utility transport with both United Nations and NATO contingents. This 845 Squadron machine, its White Ensign-adorned logo proclaiming its nationality, is manoeuvring a light field gun.

FAAM ref: S/KING 501

The Westland Merlin HAS.1, the Fleet Air Arm version of the Anglo-Italian EH–101, is the latest aircraft to join the Royal Navy. Designed to supplant the ageing Sea King, it is a larger and more powerful machine with all-weather day and night capability. It is powered by three Rolls-Royce RTM 22 engines. This example is ZF648, the fifth pre-production machine and dedicated Merlin development aircraft. The first production aircraft, ZH821, was delivered in March 1996.

FAAM ref: MERLIN 3

The eagerly-awaited HMS *Ocean*, seen fitting-out at the Kvaerner Govan shipyard on the Clyde in mid-May 1996, is the Royal Navy's first purpose-built helicopter carrier. Among the features already visible are the totally-flush flight deck, the large recesses for landing craft plus their handling davits, and some of the sponsons for light AA guns. The 666 ft (203 metre) ship, which

has a displacement of 20,500 tonnes at full load, will continue the vital amphibious support rôle pioneered in the 1960s by the *Albion* and *Bulwark*.

FAAM ref: 1996/089
Via Kvaerner Govan Ltd

# INDEX